Pathways to Well-Being

Helping Educators (and Others) Find Balance in a Connected World

Susan Brooks-Young & Sara Armstrong

International Society for Technology in Education

PORTLAND, OREGON • ARLINGTON, VA

Pathways to Well-Being
Helping Educators (and Others) Find Balance in a Connected World
Susan Brooks-Young and Sara Armstrong

Acquisitions Editor: *Valerie Witte*
Editor: *Emily Reed & Stephanie Argy*
Copy Editor: *Karstin Painter*
Proofreader: *Steffi Drewes*
Indexer: *Kento Ikeda*
Book Design and Production: *Jeff Puda*
Cover Design: *Edwin Ouellette*

Library of Congress Cataloging-in-Publication Data Available.

First Edition
ISBN: 978-1-56484-769-0
Ebook version available

Printed in the United States of America

About ISTE

The International Society for Technology in Education (ISTE) is a non-profit organization that works with the global education community to accelerate the use of technology to solve tough problems and inspire innovation. Our worldwide network believes in the potential technology holds to transform teaching and learning.

ISTE sets a bold vision for education transformation through the ISTE Standards, a framework for students, educators, administrators, coaches and computer science educators to rethink education and create innovative learning environments. ISTE hosts the annual ISTE Conference & Expo, one of the world's most influential edtech events. The organization's professional learning offerings include online courses, professional networks, year-round academies, peer-reviewed journals and other publications. ISTE is also the leading publisher of books focused on technology in education. For more information or to become an ISTE member, visit iste.org. Subscribe to ISTE's YouTube channel and connect with ISTE on Twitter, Facebook and LinkedIn.

Related ISTE Titles

To see all books available from ISTE, please visit iste.org/resources.

About the Authors

Susan Brooks-Young began her career in education teaching Head Start preschool. During the time she was in a classroom, she went on to teach every grade from kindergarten through Grade 8, and worked with high school students in after-school and summer programs in both private and public education. She also served as a site-level administrator and technology specialist in a county office of education. While readers may know Susan from the work she has done in the field of instructional technology, she has always recognized that, for the students and educators she works with to succeed, it is imperative that she approach her work keeping long-term personal development in mind.

Susan works with educators internationally. Edtech leadership, mobile technologies, digital literacy skills, and educator/student well-being are areas of particular interest for her.

Sara Armstrong is celebrating over 45 years in education. A classroom teacher for 17 years for preschool through sixth grade, she also served as principal for 11 of those years. In the early 1980s, her school participated in a telecommunications project using 300 baud modems that linked her school with another over 200 miles away. Interactive book talks via Atari 800 computers introduced Sara to the power of technology to put people in touch with others they would not ordinarily meet. From that beginning, her interest in technology has focused on bringing students and educators from around the world together to promote understanding and peace. She has worked at developing and implementing curriculum through professional development workshops and conference sessions for over 35 years.

Sara speaks at conferences on topics that include project-based learning, storytelling to build empathy, and helping children and adults ask good questions to get good answers for learning.

Contents

Foreword

I have spent much of my adult life invested in educational technology, whether that was serving as principal of a large public high school, leading innovation in the twenty-fifth largest school district in America, supporting educators across the state of Maryland, or guiding the work of ISTE as a board member. I have always valued and appreciated the insight of smart, witty, and experienced colleagues in the field. Susan and Sara are two such colleagues, and it is a pleasure to write a foreword for this important book.

I have known and collaborated with Susan for close to 20 years. We have debated educational policy, battled over the value of various technology tools, presented together, and laughed together. I deeply value her opinion and intuition. At her core, she is an educator, and she is passionate about doing what is right. Sara and I have crossed paths countless times over the years. I have heard her speak on many occasions and have used her writing to support my own work. Like Susan, Sara has been involved with educational technology since the early days, and this gives her a unique perspective to help us all find the balance and well-being in this connected world.

Susan and Sara's book provides valuable context that is deeply needed to fill a void that exists around well-being and balance in today's world. I appreciate their boldness in writing this book, and I am excited that ISTE decided to publish a work on so important a topic. Susan and Sara eloquently weave together a resource that provides a natural balance of stories, real-world connections, activities that can easily be used immediately, and references to research for those who seek even more information.

Today's teachers and parents face ever-increasing offerings of educational technology products and struggle with the appropriate balance in and out of the classroom. In *Pathways to Well-Being*, it is both powerful and refreshing to see the way many of the products our students are using in classrooms for academic purposes and at home for social reasons can be used for purposes beyond their original design and can play a critical role in supporting our collective well-being. Susan and Sara provide concrete examples of activities that use educational technology tools to support each of the themes they write about in this book. More importantly, these educational technology experts also provide non-technology options for addressing the same set of themes.

Practical and immediately applicable to the world we live in today, *Pathways to Well-Being* weaves a powerful narrative about the importance of reducing those habits that lead down a negative path and increasing connections that uplift us in our daily lives. I personally found the reflective questions in each chapter an opportunity to process in a personal way the impact my daily actions have on my well-being and on that of those closest to me. Hopefully you will take these questions and apply them to your work, home, and friendships.

As I think about my own daughters and the millions of other students growing up in a world where technology is a regular part of their lives, I realize how important it is to teach, support, and demonstrate an approach to well-being that acknowledges the critical role technology plays. Susan and Sara remind us we have a responsibility for our own well-being, and they provide solid examples, activities, and resources to support all of us in today's connected world.

   — **Ryan Imbriale** is the Executive Director of Innovative Learning with the Baltimore County Public Schools in Maryland and a former ISTE Board member.

Introduction

⟨⟩ *The great Sufi master Mullah Nasruddin* was on his hands and knees searching for something under a streetlamp. A man saw him and asked, "What are you looking for?"

"My house key," Nasruddin replied. "I lost it."

The man joined him in looking for the key, and after a period of fruitless searching, the man asked, "Are you sure you lost it around here?"

Nasruddin replied, "Oh, I didn't lose it here. I lost it over there, by my house."

"Then why," the man asked, "are you looking for it over here?"

"Because," Nasruddin said, "The light is so much better over here."

—*Mullah Nasruddin and the Lost Keys* (John, 2016)

Overview

Our purpose in writing this book is to shine a light on the topic of well-being, which leads to a life filled with balance, ease, and contentment. We all want that, but how do we get there? In this book, we reference research on a variety of topics, discuss how the focus of each chapter impacts daily life, and include activities that increase well-being in ourselves, along with a few ideas for introducing the activities to children. It starts with each of us and can spread to influence those around us in our homes, schools, communities, and ultimately throughout the world. When we work toward supporting well-being for ourselves and others, our lives are enriched immensely.

Not long ago, very few people seemed interested in well-being and the importance of resilience in dealing with stress and life's challenges. Currently, there is a trend toward making school and work environments more positive because research shows that when we can build confidence and feel we are valued, we do better work and enjoy life more.

What is your own definition of well-being? What would it take for you to feel balanced, resilient, and able to deal with whatever comes your way? If you have a strong sense of well-being, most likely you are resilient—you have the skills to help you over the bumps.

WHERE TO FIND RESOURCES ON WELL-BEING

A number of websites offer assessments and resources to promote well-being.

- **Taking Charge of Your Health and Wellbeing** (takingcharge. csh.umn.edu): This website offers a 13-question quiz to help assess your well-being on six dimensions.

- **Recipes for Wellbeing** (recipes-forwellbeing.org): Tools for supporting those interested in making positive change include diagnostic tests, links to resources, retreats, and coaching.

- **Center for Humane Technology** (humanetech.com): The problem: too much technology that alienates us from one another and manipulates us in ways of which we are not aware. The way forward: humane design.

Ephrat Livni (2018) says, "Feeling good is all fine and good, but it's fleeting. Learning to deal with difficulty, by contrast, improves your chances of feeling good again." This philosophy is echoed in the Japanese proverb, "Fall down seven times; get up eight."

Wow

According to the Psychology Today website, "Resilience is that ineffable quality that allows some people to be knocked down by life and come back stronger than ever. Rather than letting failure overcome them and drain their resolve, they find a way to rise from the ashes." When we see our mistakes as opportunities for learning and growth, when we remain optimistic and hopeful, we build our capacity for resilience—a strong aspect of well-being.

On the Taking Charge of Your Health and Wellbeing website (taking-charge.csh.umn.edu), the University of Minnesota offers a free, quick, 13-question quiz that allows you to take stock of your well-being on six dimensions: health, environment, community, relationships, security, and purpose. Each question, such as "How would you rate your ability to handle stress?" is posed on a scale running from "terrible" to "great." At the end of the survey, you can see your results and have them emailed to you. You are encouraged to work from your strengths and address any weaknesses by setting goals. There is more information regarding each topic, with suggestions for further engagement and improvement.

Each of us must determine how we will face each day. Inevitable disappointments and discouragements will occur. Through the information and activities in this book, we wish you the very best in increasing your own equanimity, reducing the stress in your life, and growing your sense of well-being.

Technology and Well-Being

Technology has made so many advances in recent years that it's hard to keep up. Devices can record our heartbeats, steps, and calories, put us in communication with people all around the world, alert us when someone is on our front porch, keep track of what's in the refrigerator, and much more. However, there are often unintended consequences of being so connected. The Center for Human Technology (humane-tech.com) sees the current use of technology as out of control, going as far as declaring, "Our society is being hijacked by technology." A provocative statement, but anyone who has observed two people—or a family, for that matter—sitting in a restaurant staring at their hand-held devices rather than talking with one another, can understand the concern behind this statement. There are things we can do, such as put our phones down when we are with someone else. We can have conversations about the use of technology tools and their effects on children, mental health, relationships, and our democracy. And we can continue to explore new technology tools in light of their value in our lives, being sure to consider their unintended consequences and effect on our well-being.

Charlotte Lieberman (n.d.) asks, "What's wrong with the way we use tech now? For one thing, it's encroaching on time we might otherwise spend doing good things for our physical and mental health." She suggests taking "tech breaks," in which we put our technology aside and focus on other things, talking with real people face to face and designating times and spaces in which technology is banned. By becoming more conscious of the influence technology tools have on our lives, we can change our practices and move toward a more balanced, healthy coexistence with them.

When ISTE first undertook to create technology standards for students, educators, and administrators, the focus was on being able to use the tools themselves. Currently, much more emphasis is placed on how and why to use these tools, as well as their effects on us. This change in emphasis reflects the ongoing concern for digital age skills that include collaboration, communication, critical thinking, and creativity. This book specifically supports the ISTE Standards for Educators and Education Leaders, particularly the Equity and Citizenship Advocate standard (Education Leaders) and Citizen standard (Educators). We include references to specific standards at the end of chapters 1 through 6, and they are available online (iste.org/standards).

Our technology tools can certainly enhance our lives, if we are thoughtful about their use. We hope considering the unexpected consequences of technology use can help us decrease our harmful habits and increase positive connections, which ultimately will lead to enhanced well-being.

The Layout

This introduction is followed by seven chapters, the last of which is a conclusion. Chapters 1 through 6 address a particular component of well-being, and those chapters all follow a similar format:

- **An introductory story** sets the stage for the topic that will be explored in the chapter.

- **The Overview** introduces that chapter's topic and lays the groundwork for its contribution to your well-being. Sidebars provide information about applicable ISTE Standards for Educators and Education Leaders, and about where to find additional research on that chapter's topic.

- **The Real-World Connection** moves from "Okay, I now understand the topic better," to answer application questions such as, "How does the topic relate to everyday life?" or "What can I do to incorporate what I have learned into both my professional and personal spheres of influence to make my life—and the lives of those around me—better?"

- **Technology** can help or hinder our efforts. Technology tools are not inherently good or bad; it's what we do with them that counts. In each chapter, we describe positive and negative aspects of technology related to the topic at hand.

- **Activities** sections suggest eight ways you can move toward incorporating new behaviors into your daily life. The activities are primarily designed to be completed alone, but occasionally a partner or group might be recommended. Sidebars add ideas for adapting and enhancing the activities for youngsters.

- **Questions for Reflection** challenge you to take what you've read and make it your own. What will you do to further your understanding of the topic? How will you use what you've learned to increase your well-being?

- **Additional Resources** cites research through articles, books, and websites on the topic.

The Content

We hope all of the chapters have information and activities that speak to you and help you create your own path to greater well-being. Feel free to move around, dipping into different chapters as you will.

Introduction
This chapter sets the context of the book and suggests the importance of balance, resilience, and well-being as aspects of a life well-lived.

Chapter 1: **Gratitude**
There are many things for which to be grateful. The benefits to becoming aware of them and focusing on them rather than on the unpleasant things that might also occur increase health and well-being.

Chapter 2: **Being Positive**
If we can recognize the positive things that happen every day, and train ourselves to more readily see the good in our lives (as opposed to the negative), we can expand our mindsets and engender more positive experiences in our lives. These lead to a more positive outlook, and a self-fulfilling prophecy of positivity.

Chapter 3: **Getting Focused**
Considering the upsides and downsides of daydreaming and dealing with distractions helps us develop strategies for focusing on the tasks at hand—in concert with tending to our own well-being.

Chapter 4: **Empathy**
Being able to put oneself in another's shoes benefits both parties. We can build strong relationships—which research shows have more health benefits than we might have believed—and understand others in important ways.

Chapter 5: **Kindness**
Being kind to yourself and others may seem easy, or even irrelevant. However, research shows the benefits of conscious acts of kindness include stress reduction, reducing blood pressure, easing anxiety, and releasing "feel good" hormones (Proctor, n.d.). Information and activities in this chapter expand these ideas.

Chapter 6: **Movement**

Small movements, large movements: going to the gym, playing sports, or simply taking short breaks to walk outdoors all benefit our health and well-being in important ways. Technology can help—and hinder—these efforts.

Chapter 7: **Where to Go from Here**

The concluding chapter of the book brings together the research and strategies we have explored into a call to action. What will you do to increase your well-being? How might you commit to adding activities to your daily life in a meaningful way? Can you use technology to assist in these efforts, while keeping in mind the unexpected consequences or challenges that technology use might bring?

We suggest you take a look at the table of contents and start with the topic most interesting to you. We have found that people often are drawn to the chapter on gratitude first because it seems to have the greatest impact with the least amount of effort. However, start where you like, and move around within the book as you see fit. We sincerely hope you will take some of the ideas and activities from this book and increase your well-being through your interests.

Additional Resources

"How to Be Resilient: Eight Steps to Success When Life Gets Hard," *TIME*, Eric Barker, July 18, 2014. tinyurl.com/nb94f39

"Is Social Connection the Best Path to Happiness?" *Greater Good Magazine*, Kira M. Newman, June 27, 2018. tinyurl.com/ybkw2ar5

"Resilience Is About How You Recharge, Not How You Endure," *Harvard Business Review*, Shawn Achor and Michelle Gielan, June 24, 2016. tinyurl.com/h4m7wmb

1

Gratitude

〰 *On January 1, 2012,* a young man named Brian Doyle and two of his friends had a near miss with a wrong-way driver. One year later, Brian shared his story at the TEDxYouth@SanDiego 2013 event. He explained that this near accident impacted his life in an unexpected way: For nearly a year he thought about people in his life and ways they had influenced him. Then, over the 2012 Thanksgiving holiday, he decided to say thank you to one person every day for the next 365 days. He began the next day. From his best friend to former classmates and teachers, from his parents and other family members to people he barely knew, Brian took the time to say thank you. He learned many lessons from saying thank you, but one of the most important was that people do not know how much they are appreciated by others—especially if no one ever tells them. He also reported that his focus shifted to looking for the positives in every day instead of the negative (Doyle, 2014).

Overview

It's no accident that we've chosen to begin this book with the topic of gratitude. If you decide to try the strategies suggested in this book, start with gratitude. Why? Personal experience has shown us that the simple act of expressing gratitude is the quickest way to increase our sense of well-being, and experts in the field agree. They identify a number of immediate and long-term benefits of experiencing and expressing gratitude, even after engaging in this practice for only a short period of time. What are the benefits, and how do you get started? Let's begin by establishing a common understanding of what we mean by *gratitude*.

People often define gratitude as being thankful for someone or something, but it is more than that. Gratitude is also people's willingness to show appreciation for kindnesses extended to them and to return or pass along that kindness in some way. In other words, initially, gratitude is experienced internally, but it is enhanced or expanded when we externally express thanks to someone or are inspired to perform acts of kindness of our own. This twofold definition is what we mean when using the term *gratitude*.

The importance of gratitude has been recognized for centuries. For example, Aesop (620–564 BCE) said, "Gratitude is the sign of noble souls," and Marcus Tullius Cicero (106–43 BCE) reportedly

WHERE TO FIND RESOURCES ON GRATITUDE

Interested in learning more about how practicing gratitude changes lives? Check out these web resources for research on gratitude:

Expanding the Science and Practice of Gratitude
(ggsc.berkeley.edu): Housed at the University of California, Berkeley, the Greater Good Science Center sponsors research and public initiatives that focus on gratitude. Access articles and other information on the website.

"Five Best Books on Gratitude + Oliver Sacks' Gratitude Book"
(positivepsychologyprogram.com/gratitude-books-oliver-sachs): Five book recommendations as well as links to additional readings on gratitude.

"Five Steps for Building Grateful Kids" (cct.biola.edu/5-steps-building-grateful-kids): This article by Jeffrey J. Froh discusses why it is important to teach kids to be grateful. It features five strategies to encourage kids to have more gratitude.

said, "Gratitude is not only the greatest of virtues, but the parent of all the others." The positive benefits of practicing gratitude are numerous. For simplicity's sake, we have classified benefits into three areas: physical health, mental health, and social health. Let's take a brief look at benefits in each of these categories.

Physical Health

Robert A. Emmons, PhD, author and professor of psychology at University of California, Davis, focuses on gratitude in his work. Based on results of several studies, Emmons' research team found that people of all ages who nourish feelings of gratitude see health benefits in as little as three weeks. These benefits include: a more robust immune system; reduced risk of heart disease due to physical changes such as decreased blood pressure; less stress; and fewer aches and pains in general (Emmons, 2010).

It also appears that people who feel grateful take better care of themselves. For example, they are more likely to exercise regularly and have healthier diets. These people also sleep more deeply and feel better rested on waking.

Mental Health

Dr. Emmons and other researchers identify several ways gratitude improves individuals' mental health. For example, people who show gratitude experience an increase in their sense of personal happiness at home and at work while also reporting a decrease in emotions such as envy, depression, or anxiety (Emmons, 2010). Similar findings were identified in two studies that focused on expressing gratitude in writing, for example by journaling or writing a letter. The subjects of one study were health care practitioners working in high stress environments while subjects of the second study were people participating in therapy. Participants in both studies reported decreased mental stress and increases in their mental health after keeping gratitude diaries or journals or, in the second study, writing letters of gratitude (American Psychiatric Association, 2017).

There are additional mental health benefits connected to gratitude. They include increased optimism, better performance both professionally and academically, and a greater ability to cope with difficult circumstances. In fact, a team of researchers led by Dr. Barbara L. Fredrickson was exploring a hypothesis that positive emotions foster resiliency when they tested a group of college students in early 2001 to measure the level of positive emotions they expressed—including gratitude. These same students were tested in the weeks following the 9/11 attacks in New York City. In analyzing students' pre- and post-9/11 scores, researchers found that those participants who had expressed higher levels of positive emotions, including gratitude, were less likely to experience depression or other negative emotions following the events of 9/11 (Fredrickson et al., 2003).

Social Health

Based upon the give-and-take nature of fully expressed gratitude, researchers at UC Davis identified a connection between gratitude and a person's social health. For starters, people who are grateful also tend to be empathetic—very good at putting themselves in someone else's shoes. Along with their ability to empathize, grateful people tend to have a strong sense of community and believe they have a responsibility to care for others. These characteristics lead to positive outcomes, including:

- **Deep friendships**
- **The ability to be good team players**
- **Strong family relationships**
- **Willingness to help others**
- **Strong sense of community**

The Real-World Connection

Americans' levels of optimism and happiness have been declining over the last few years. An Allstate/*National Journal* Heartland Monitor Poll conducted in 2015 asked participants how six current social and economic trends in American society impacted their general feelings of optimism or pessimism. While two of the trends made them feel more optimistic, participants reported that the remaining four trends left them feeling increasingly pessimistic (Brownstein, 2015). Additionally, America's ranking in the international World Happiness Report has fallen for the second time in two years. In the 2018 report, America fell from 14th to 18th in the report's ranking of 156 countries from around the world (Horton, 2018). The good news is that individuals can make small efforts to recognize what they have to be grateful for and move toward more positive feelings and actions. The better news is that one person can encourage others, both directly and indirectly, to spread feelings of gratitude throughout their own spheres of influence.

OTHER PEOPLE (handwritten annotation)

A classic example of this phenomenon is found in Eleanor H. Porter's time-honored children's novel from 1913, *Pollyanna*. An orphaned child (the title character) comes to live with her aunt, who is a cold, unhappy person. During the course of the story, Pollyanna changes not only her aunt's view of the world but that of many townspeople through her ability to express gratitude and practice kindness. The profound impact of these changes is realized when Pollyanna is temporarily paralyzed following an accident and those whose lives she has touched rally to help her find the good in this terrible event.

A bit corny, perhaps, but intentional focus on expressing gratitude helps not only the individual but everyone with whom that person interacts. Just one person can influence others by practicing gratitude quietly and consistently. In turn, those who pick up on this "attitude of gratitude" will influence their families and friends as well. Give it a try!

Technology and Gratitude

The idiom "keeping up with the Joneses" comes from the title of a comic strip created by Arthur R. Momand and published in several U.S. newspapers from 1913 to 1938. The strip depicted the lives of the McGinis family, who measured their own level of social and material successes by comparing themselves to their neighbors, the Joneses, who never actually appeared in the strip. Needless to say, the McGinises continually struggled to measure up (Pritchard, 2013).

Being envious of others is part of the human condition, but it is also fair to say that since the early days of readily available, inexpensive print materials, mass media has helped intensify these feelings of jealousy. Technologies—including movies, radio, television, and now the internet—make it even easier to experience discontent with our lives. Although the internet alone cannot be blamed solely for anyone's sense of dissatisfaction, it is reasonable to acknowledge that all forms of media can contribute to a person's discontent when not viewed with a critical eye.

Why does this happen? There are exceptions, but most people who post on social media do not air their dirty laundry so publicly. They usually focus on the high points in their lives—vacations, weddings, holiday celebrations, and so on. These upbeat, on-top-of-the-world messages can give readers the sense that their own lives are not nearly as positive or rewarding as those of their friends; this can lead to lower self-esteem and a sense of dissatisfaction (Barr, 2018). Instead of being grateful for all the good things and people that are already part of their lives, they develop resentments about what they think they should have, but do not.

Spot on explanation of how FB makes me feel

The way to combat the drive to keep up with the virtual Joneses is to step back and think critically about what's happening and why. Here are a few things to try with social media feeds and other online accounts.

1. **Unfollow people who arouse jealousy.** You know who they are. No matter what they write about, you end up feeling inferior because you believe your life will never measure up to theirs. It does not matter if others consider these people inspirational—if you do not, unfollow them. Whether it's people you know in real life or online, they'll never know you are not reading their posts, and you will feel better.

2. **Follow people who inspire you,** people whose posts lift you up or offer content that resonates with you. Perhaps they have expertise in something you'd like to learn more about, or they handle life's ups and downs with humor and grace. Whether they make you smile or get you thinking, these posts will not invoke the green-eyed monster.

3. **Log out of your social media accounts.** Did you know that the average person spends 116 minutes on social media per day? That's nearly two hours! (Asano, 2017) If you're feeling over-whelmed or like you can't keep up with everything you need to get done, this may be a contributing factor. We're not suggesting that you give up social media, only that you make it a little more cumbersome to check your feeds. When it takes a mere click of a button to peek at Instagram, Facebook, Twitter, LinkedIn, or

whatever social media platforms you use, it's all too easy to fall down the social media rabbit hole whenever you get bored. Simply spending less time reading posts can lift your spirits.

4. **Turn off notifications.** If you cannot bring yourself to log out of your accounts, at least turn off notifications. It's nearly impossible to ignore the Facebook Messenger chime or the ding that lets you know someone has liked or retweeted one of your tweets or sent you an email.

5. **Spend more offline time with people.** Social media is not a replacement for face-to-face relationships. Yes, you still might make unrealistic comparisons of your life to the lives of those around you, but real-life encounters include visual and aural cues that help you maintain a better perspective on interactions.

6. **Fight the Fear of Missing Out (FOMO).** When a post you see online makes you feel as though you are missing out because you do not have (or have not done) something, take a moment to think about your reaction. Specifically, what are you feeling and why? If you can name the emotions you are experiencing and figure out why they bother you, it's possible to change your focus from what you do not have to what you might want to do.

Can social media and other technologies be used to enhance your sense of gratitude? Absolutely! For example, you can:

1. Use digital photos and a collage-maker app to create a virtual poster of people, places, or things you are grateful for. Use it as wallpaper for your laptop, smartphone, or tablet.

2. Subscribe to blogs or sites that suggest daily practices for expressing gratitude, and implement suggestions that appeal to you.

3. Use email or messaging to reach out and thank someone.

4. Make a video call using FaceTime, Facebook Live, Skype, or another video-calling app to connect in real time with someone and share a little gratitude.

5. Make a gratitude video to share with family and friends.

Technology does not replace face-to-face relationships, but it can be used to enhance them.

Activities

Here are several activities you can choose from to help you focus on gratitude. Some work well for personal use (e.g., the gratitude journal), while others are great for group use (e.g., the wall of gratitude). The first six activities can easily be used with kids in a variety of settings with little or no modifications. In addition, the sidebar includes web resources that can be used to enhance activities 1 and 2.

1. **Gratitude journal:** One tried-and-true activity is keeping a gratitude journal. Use each entry to identify three things for which you are grateful. These can be stated in broad terms, such as "my health" or "my family," but they may also identify very specific things, such as "completing my project on time." Take a few minutes to explain why each item listed inspires your gratitude. Research shows that weekly writing is enough to increase a person's sense of well-being, but more frequent entries have an even greater impact. Daily journaling is optimal.

2. **Gratitude displays:** You've probably heard of vision boards that people create to illustrate what they want in their lives. Instead of focusing on what you want, create a display that illustrates all the things and people in your life you are grateful for already having. It might be a bulletin board, a poster-board collage, or a collection of knick-knacks that hold special meaning. Whatever it is, surround yourself with images or objects that remind you of specific reasons for your gratitude.

3. **Gratitude jar:** Each morning, write something for which you are grateful on a slip of paper, and drop it into a decorative jar or box. Those days when you're feeling a little down or cannot think of something to write, take a few slips from the jar and read them to spark an idea about something you can be grateful for that day.

4. **No complaints:** Imagine that 48 terrific things and two negative things happen during your day. Do you focus on the fact that 96% of your day was great, or is your attention riveted on the 4% that did not go so well? If you're like most people, you pay greater attention to the negative. Of course there are times when negative events supersede the positive, but most negative occurrences consume our attention because we have taught ourselves to ignore the positives in our lives. One way to develop an attitude of gratitude

is to break this habit by declaring "No Complaints" days. Vow to spend a day focusing on what's right with your life, not what's gone wrong. At the end of the day, reflect on how you feel. Do you notice a difference?

5. **Thank-you notes:** A heartfelt verbal thank you covers many occasions, but there are times when more formal acknowledgment is needed. Most people appreciate the extra effort required to write a thank-you note, address and stamp it, and drop it into a mailbox. The next time you want to let someone know you are grateful for

---

Activity ❶   GRATITUDE JOURNALS: Online Tools

- **Penzu Online Journals** (penzu.com/gratitude-journal): Penzu offers free, secure online journals for a variety of uses. Optional mobile apps make your online journal available on any device. The website discusses gratitude journals, their purpose, and tips to get started. There are also links to templates for readers who prefer recommended formats.

- **Online Word Processors:** Tools such as Google Docs (docs.google.com) or Microsoft 365 (office.com) are also fine for keeping private journals. You can create your own format or look at the templates linked to the Penzu journal tool above to get some ideas.

- **Kids' Gratitude Journals:** If you ask kids to write gratitude journals, you'll need to consider privacy issues and use composition books instead of writing online. Of course, if your school is a GAFE (Google Apps for Education) or Microsoft 365 school, students younger than 13 have permission to use online word processors.

Activity ❷   GRATITUDE DISPLAYS: Online Tools

In addition to the gratitude display formats suggested in the first activity description, you might consider a digital display. There are several tools that make it easy to create and share digital posters that include text, images, audio and video. Here are a couple tried-and-true online tools:

- **Poster Maker** (postermaker.com): This free basic tool allows you to create posters using clip art provided or upload your own images. You may save an image of your poster to print or share online.

- **ThingLink** (thinglink.com): Free and premium accounts available. Use ThingLink to create hyperlinked digital posters; add text, audio, video, and images to enhance the display.

something he or she has done, take the time to write and mail—or even hand deliver—a note.

6. **Volunteer:** Giving back to someone else is a meaningful way to express gratitude for being in a position to help someone else. There are innumerable ways to help others, from occasional activities (such as hosting food drives) to ongoing commitments (such as leading youth groups or visiting homebound neighbors). Even when your time is limited, opportunities to be helpful are plentiful; you only need to recognize and act on them.

7. **Practice self-care:** Self-indulgence is the excessive gratification of personal desires—behavior that is not particularly admirable. Self-care, on the other hand, consists of activities designed to increase our health and well-being. Taking care of oneself is an inward expression of gratitude, a way we can demonstrate self-respect and esteem. Think about things you already do that fall under the category of self-care. Is this a regular practice for you, or could you up the ante a bit? If possible, do at least one kind thing for yourself on a daily basis.

8. **Brighten someone's day:** Have you ever worked a job where you relied on tips to earn minimum wage? We have! As a result, we tend to be very generous when tipping wait staff, cab drivers, and others who depend on tips to make a living. Of course, a "thank you" is always appreciated, but—when appropriate, and if you can afford it—a substantial tip can make a big difference in someone's day.

Questions for Reflection

1. What role does gratitude play in your sense of well-being?

2. What daily acts of gratitude can you cultivate in your life?

3. How do you currently express gratitude to family members and friends?

4. What is one way you can use technology to express gratitude to yourself or others?

5. What will you do today to express gratitude to yourself or others?

Additional Resources

"Gratitude: The Most Effective Social Media Practice," Carol Bush, February 1, 2016. thesocialnurse.com/gratitude-the-most-effective-social-media-practice

"In Praise of Gratitude," *Healthbeat,* Harvard Health Publishing, November, 2011. health.harvard.edu/newsletter_article/in-praise-of-gratitude

Making grateful kids: The science of building character, Jeffrey Froh and Giacomo Bono, 2014. West Conshohoken, PA: Templeton Press.

"Pessimism, Optimism; Definite, Indefinite: Societies According to Peter Thiel," Zak Slayback, October, 2014. tinyurl.com/ycfa3na2

"Seven Scientifically Proven Benefits of Gratitude," *Psychology Today,* Amy Morin, April 3, 2015. tinyurl.com/jne45sx

"Social Media's Impact on Self-Esteem," *HuffPost,* Clarissa Silva, February 22, 2017. tinyurl.com/y832dm9a

"You've Heard Gratitude Is Good for You. Here's What Science Says," Michael T. Murray, March, 2015. tinyurl.com/y8nmrcxv

ISTE Standards Connection

ISTE Standards for Educators 3a: Create experiences for learners to make positive, socially responsible contributions and exhibit empathetic behavior online that build relationships and community.

ISTE Standards for Education Leaders 1c: Model digital citizenship by critically evaluating online resources, engaging in civil discourse online, and using digital tools to contribute to positive social change.

ISTE Standards for Education Leaders 3d: Support educators in using technology to advance learning that meets the diverse learning, cultural, and social–emotional needs of individual students.

When adults regularly talk with children about the differences between life as depicted in the media and in the real world, they are able to help them remember that television, movies, social media, and other forms of online entertainment are not necessarily accurate representations of how most people live. Educators and others who work with children are uniquely positioned to help them use online resources and digital tools in healthy, responsible ways.

Being Positive

✺ Consider the following well-known parable.

A man and his grandson were talking one day. The grand-father was trying to help his grandson grapple with how the negative and positive elements that surround us in life impact how we live. He told his grandson that he was experiencing a mighty internal battle between two wolves. One wolf represented all the negativity in the world while the other wolf represented everything positive and good in the world.

"Which wolf will win, Grandfather?" asked the boy.

"The one I choose to feed," replied the grandfather.

HUGE –
–feed the one you
want to win

Overview

Somewhere along the way, the idea of cultivating positive thinking as a strategy for increasing life satisfaction has been dismissed. We suspect that may be due, at least in part, to pop-psychology gurus who preach that all a person needs to do to succeed is visualize what they want—usually something material—and then think happy thoughts. There are also people who decide that embracing positivity means never having to deal with unhappiness, hurt, anger, and other negative emotions that touch everyone's lives. When we write about positivity, we are focusing on the general benefits of having a positive or optimistic attitude in life overall. We are not encouraging you to avoid pain by exhibiting a giddy persona or expecting material gain via happy thoughts.

So, what is a more down-to-earth definition of positive psychology? According to the Psychology Today website, positive psychology "emphasizes traits, thinking patterns, behaviors, and experiences that are forward-thinking and can help improve the quality of a person's day-to-day life. . . . It is an exploration of one's strengths, rather than one's weaknesses" (n.d.). In other words, positive psychology helps people learn how to be optimistic yet realistic, to strengthen individuals' abilities to persevere, think creatively, develop spiritually, and more. When we encourage people to recognize the positive aspects of their lives, we are suggesting they try looking at events through a new lens, not that they numb themselves to their feelings.

A Couple of Theories

Keep your thoughts positive, because your thoughts become your words. Keep your words positive, because your words become your behavior. Keep your behavior positive, because your behavior becomes your habits. Keep your habits positive, because your habits become your values. Keep your values positive, because your values become your destiny. —Mahatma Gandhi, (as qtd. Gold, 2002)

Broaden-and-Build Theory

Barbara Fredrickson, Kenan distinguished professor at University of North Carolina at Chapel Hill, would agree with Gandhi that positivity impacts people's lives. Fredrickson's research leads her to the position that positive emotions make it possible for people to open their minds and hearts to possibilities they might not recognize otherwise. Her studies also find that positive people are more resilient than negative people, students who are experiencing positive emotions perform better on academic tests, and positive people are more likely to look past differences to recognize common ground in a variety of settings (Fredrickson, 2011).

About 20 years ago, Fredrickson developed the broaden-and-build theory, which suggests that positive emotions broaden one's perspective and encourage novel or creative approaches to life's challenges, while negative emotions typically cause people to narrow their focus, as when they feel threatened (e.g., fight or flight reactions). Furthermore, people who have experienced the immediate benefits of positive emotions are more likely to build reserves they can draw on when facing difficult situations in the future.

In 2004, Fredrickson published a study that included five findings. She wrote then that positive emotions:

1. broaden thought–action strategies;

2. undo lingering negative emotions;

3. fuel psychological resiliency;

4. build personal resources; and

5. support psychological and physical well-being.

WHERE TO FIND RESEARCH ON BEING POSITIVE

Interested in learning more about how being positive changes lives? Check out these websites to research optimism:

- *"Optimism and Its Impact on Mental and Physical Well-Being"* (ncbi.nlm.nih.gov/pmc/articles/PMC2894461): This article is hosted on the U.S. National Library of Medicine, National Institutes of Health website and offers an overview of multiple studies that explore how positivity affects mental and physical health.

- *Hope & Optimism* (hopeoptimism.com/): This four-year project at Cornell, University of Pennsylvania, and Notre Dame explored the impact of hope and optimism. Videos, research, and other resources are available on the website.

- *Learned Optimism: How to Change Your Mind and Your Life* (goodreads.com/book/show/26123.Learned_Optimism): This book by Martin E. P. Seligman explains how optimism enhances lives, and that anyone can learn how to practice optimism.

The point of this theory is not to fake positive emotions, but to recognize that positive emotions bring rewards in the short and long term. So, when good things are happening, appreciate those things, and regularly engage in activities likely to increase your sense of positivity.

The PERMA Model

Martin Seligman, who is sometimes referred to as the father of positive psychology, developed the PERMA model. The acronym, PERMA, is based on the five elements of the model which Seligman identified as promoting life satisfaction:

- **P**ositive Emotion—having a positive outlook on life.

- **E**ngagement—finding and participating in an absorbing hobby or pastime.

- **R**elationships—having a strong support network made up of family members and friends.

- **M**eaning—identifying a purpose or reason for life.

- **A**ccomplishments—setting and achieving meaningful goals, (Pascha, 2017).

What we want to point out here is that, of the five elements, only one speaks directly to personally experiencing positive emotions. The remaining four identify behaviors and connections that lead to meaningful, purpose-filled lives. Implementing this model requires more effort than pasting a smile on your face or avoiding serious aspects of living.

The Real-World Connection

According to the 2017 Harris Poll Survey of American Happiness, respondents report being happier than they were in 2016. Before you jump to conclusions, you need to know that in 2016, 31% reported being happy; in 2017, the number increased to 33%. Hardly anything to get excited about when you realize only one in three Americans surveyed identifies as happy. It is also important to know that American participants have rated their level of happiness in the low- to mid-thirties percentage every year since the survey began in 2008. The survey does not ask questions that might explain why Americans do not appear to consider themselves very happy (Sifferlin, 2017).

We do not fare much better these days in the World Happiness Report. As far as members of the Organization for Economic Cooperation and Development (OECD) are concerned, we have fallen from the third-happiest nation in 2007 to the eighteenth-happiest nation in 2018. A full chapter in the 2017 report is devoted to explaining America's decline in happiness, suggesting that, "The United States can and should raise happiness by addressing America's multifaceted social crisis—rising inequality, corruption, isolation, and distrust—rather than focusing exclusively or even mainly on economic growth, especially since the concrete proposals along these lines would exacerbate rather than ameliorate the deepening social crisis" (Helliwell et al., 2017).

Consider the basis of Fredrickson's broaden-and-build theory, or the five elements of Seligman's PERMA model, and take another look at the recommendations for Americans in the 2017 World Happiness Report. The things people could do to alleviate isolation, distrust, inequality—and even corruption—correlate to the elements in PERMA, which align with the outcomes identified in broaden-and-build. Not coincidentally, respondents in the Harris poll also reported that they are distracted and feel out of control. They seldom engage in activities they enjoy (e.g., hobbies) and seem to have decreasing amounts of free time (Sifferlin, 2017). All the more reason to take time to fully engage in enjoyable activities, pay attention to your relationships, find reason and purpose in your life, and set achievable life goals. The Activities section in this chapter offers eight things you can do right away to engage in behaviors that will increase your own positivity.

Technology and Positivity

Stories abound about the negative impact of misuse or overuse of technology: It often leads to injured relationships, a sense of purposelessness, and limited or no feelings of accomplishment. These outcomes typically lead to damaged feelings. In her TED talk, "Connected, but Alone?" Sherry Turkle (2012) contends that not only does technology have the potential to change *what* we do, it can also change *who* we are. She cites the numbers of people who now text surreptitiously (or openly) during activities such as meetings, gatherings of friends, mealtimes, even funerals, when it is far more appropriate to be focusing on the people we are with or what is happening around us. She calls this a way to be together without actually being together.

Turkle's research suggests that many people use technology to avoid developing deep face-to-face relationships. The downside is that people feel disconnected from one another, that they are not being heard, and they are right! This is not a problem caused by the technological device itself, but by how we choose to use it. Turkle also notes that social media makes it possible for us to present polished, carefully edited versions of our lives because so many of our interactions on platforms like Facebook or Twitter are asynchronous. We have time to think about what we want to say, edit it if we do not like how it sounds, or manipulate photos before we post them. There are times when having that space to carefully consider how we want to present ourselves is useful, but face-to-face interactions cannot be so carefully orchestrated. We need to carry on real-time, genuine conversations, though they may require more of us than online interactions.

There's a lot more to why social media interactions are more appealing to many people than real-time interactions and yet less satisfying in the long run, but you get the idea. When we hide behind devices to avoid talking with people who are physically present, we need to think about what we are doing, and why.

So, how can we use technology to experience positive emotions? Think about the statement above—devices in and of themselves do not cause problems; it is how we choose to use those devices that can be problematic. If that is truly the case, what are ways we can use technology that would result in positive outcomes? Here are a few simple yet effective ideas.

1. **Keep up with family members.** It is not unusual for families to be scattered around the globe. Until recently, this separation almost always meant family ties broke down as time and distance took their toll. Today, this does not have to be the case. Social media, live chat, and other online tools make it a snap to stay connected to the people we love, no matter where in the world they might be. This is particularly helpful for staying in touch with extended family members.

2. **Reconnect with friends.** People tend to stay in touch with a few of their closest friends, while losing contact with people they like but have to work harder to stay connected with. Social media and other tools can be leveraged to maintain communication in these types of friendships. These may not be your best friends, but they still enrich your life in meaningful ways.

3. **Online tutorials.** Recently, Susan needed to purchase a replacement bulb for one of the taillights on her car. She blithely assumed someone at the auto parts store would know how to install the new bulb, but she was wrong. Not to be deterred, she whipped out her smartphone and found a video tutorial that presented step-by-step directions for replacing the bulb. Not only did she walk away feeling empowered, but the store clerk learned a helpful job-related skill as well! Online tutorials allow people to take positive actions in what might otherwise be disappointing circumstances.

4. **Online therapy.** Many people live in rural areas where access to mental health services is limited or nonexistent. Telepsychology is a growing field that offers inexpensive, convenient access to mental health service providers. Of course, it is important to carefully vet providers, but this can be a real boon for people in remote parts of the country.

5. **Family safety plans.** If you live in an area prone to hurricanes, tornadoes, earthquakes, or other natural disasters, you know the importance of developing a plan for family members to connect with one another during, or after, such an event. Share safety information with students and their families and suggest they develop a plan. Here are four technology-based tips from the American Red Cross website (2018) to help get you started:

   a. Call during off-peak hours for the best chance of getting through.

   b. Send a text message, which may go through when phone calls cannot.

   c. Check your loved one's social media pages (i.e., Facebook, Twitter), as they may have already gone online to tell their story.

   d. Send an email.

Technology does not replace face-to-face relationships but can be used to enhance them.

Activities

Here are several activities to help you look at life with a more positive attitude. All of these activities lend themselves well to personal use. They also support the kinds of interpersonal skills we want to foster in kids. It's possible to introduce the activity concepts through direct instruction, but the real power behind these activities occurs when adults consistently model these behaviors. The sidebar includes resources that can be used to enhance activities 1 and 2.

1. **Accentuate the positive:** Things happen to, or around, people every single day. Some are pleasant, some not so much. It probably comes as no surprise that most people tend to focus on the negative events in their day, rather than the positive things. You can change that with a little practice. At the end of each day, take a few minutes to identify and write about one to three positive events that took place. Briefly explain why these happenings were constructive. In as few as three weeks, people who make this a daily practice report reduced stress and increased physical well-being.

2. **Future story:** A future story is one you create to help you imagine something in your future. It can be something that will happen in the short term, or something you expect to happen down the road. The more details you are able to include, the easier it will be to visualize. That, in turn, makes it easier for you to do the things necessary to make the story come true. When Susan skied regularly, she created future stories where she visualized mastering a particularly difficult run. She would talk herself through what she would do while skiing the run; when she actually was there, she skied better than she had previously! When you decide on your future story, write a narrative, a letter to yourself, or reflection. Be sure to write as though you have already accomplished your goal.

3. **The worst thing:** People spend a lot of time worrying about things that are either out of their control or unlikely to happen. The next time you find yourself fixating on a concern that falls into one of

Activity ❶   ACCENTUATE THE POSITIVE: Online Tools

You may want to keep track of the positive events you notice in an online journal like those mentioned in chapter 1, activity 1. However, if keeping a journal is not your thing, consider tracking your daily positive events using a digital sticky note tool like Google Keep (keep.google.com). Available as a Chrome app for computers and laptops, as well as Android and iOS mobile devices, Google Keep allows users to create and organize sticky notes where they can add text, make lists, and even add images. In the case of noting positive experiences, you can create a sticky note for the week, add to it daily, then at the end of the week, save the list to a Google Doc to keep a running record of positive experiences over time.

An alternative to Google Keep is Lino (en.linoit.com). This free, easy-to-use tool works with a web browser as well as in apps for iOS and Android. Create multiple canvases where you can save sticky notes and images.

Activity ❷   FUTURE STORIES: Online Tools

When you think about crafting a story, you do not necessarily need to write it down. Hard copies may be the best solution for stories you plan to share with others, but future stories are private, not necessarily meant to be shared. Instead of writing down your future story, consider preserving it as an audio recording. This works because the point of a future story is to talk to yourself as though you have already achieved a goal or solved a tricky situation. Computers, laptops, and mobile devices typically come with a free voice recorder installed. In Windows, the tool is called Voice Recorder, and on Macs, use Quick Time Player. To record audio on a mobile device, check the corresponding app store to find a free recording app.

these two categories, try this strategy. Identify what you are worried about. For example, you are asked to be at a meeting where you know an unpleasant person will also attend. Ask yourself what's the worst thing that could happen if you are confronted by this person (e.g., you will be put on the defensive). Then identify the worst thing that might happen in that case (e.g., you will be embarrassed in front of others). Repeat this step two or three times. You will soon realize that, in most cases, you will be able to handle virtually any situation.

4. **Find the silver lining:** While it may seem syrupy sweet, it is possible to find some good in nearly any event. An extreme example of this may be found in a psychotherapeutic method called logotherapy, developed by Viktor Frankl. In his book, *Man's Search for Meaning*, Frankl wrote about his experience as an inmate in a Nazi concentration camp during World War II. He came to believe that his survival as a prisoner depended on his ability to identify his purpose in life, something he could feel positive about, and then to imagine the outcome of achieving that purpose (Frankl, 1985). Thankfully, most of us will never face that level of trauma in our lives, but there will still be negative situations that can devastate us unless we are able to reframe the situation. When faced with an event that seems insurmountable, work on changing your perspective by asking questions such as, "What can I learn from this situation?" or "How can I strengthen my personal relationships because of what has happened?" Finding the silver lining can make a huge difference in your ability to maintain a positive outlook on life.

5. **Self-talk:** What kinds of things do you say to yourself when you are unhappy or upset? Do you give yourself a pep talk, or do you berate yourself for being stupid or inept? If it's the latter, please rethink what you are doing. We are not suggesting that people can (or even should) be happy all the time. However, positive self-talk does reduce stress, increases self-confidence, and leads to better relationships with others. Next time you're tempted to come down hard on yourself, try some positive self-talk. It will help!

6. **Reading between the lines:** Everyone does it. A friend or family member says something like, "Who gave you that haircut?" or "You look tired." Next thing you know, you are consumed with trying to interpret the negative message behind what was said. Instead of assuming the worst, try this approach instead. Pause for a moment and ask yourself if your negative reaction is warranted. If not, let it go. If so, gently ask the other person to clarify what she or he said (avoid demanding remarks such as, "What did you mean by that?"). By not immediately assuming that the people around you are out to get you, you will find that your relationships are happier and healthier.

7. **Positive language:** Words matter. Listen to yourself and those around you carefully. What do you hear? Are your conversations focused on positive topics, or are they consistently peppered with negative remarks? When you frame conversations, how do you use words to influence listeners' thinking? For example, would you say that Tamiflu is effective in reducing the number of patients who develop pneumonia as a result of having the flu by 44%, or would you say that 56% of people who have the flu will develop pneumonia even if they take Tamiflu? Both statements are true, but one is more likely to encourage someone with flu to take Tamiflu than the other. Be more aware of the words you and those around you use. They make a difference in your worldview.

8. **Create hope:** People who have a positive outlook on life also have hope. In fact, it is one of the hallmark traits of positive people. That does not mean that they are naïve or cling to false hopes—hopeful people set achievable, realistic goals they can actually meet. One way to help create a more hopeful world is to help others feel hopeful. For example, use a site like Kiva (kiva.org) to fund microloans designed to help people start businesses. Or, closer to home, make a practice of letting family members and friends know you care about them and are thinking of them. Lifting someone's spirits is a great way to create hope.

Questions for Reflection

1. What role does positivity play in your sense of life satisfaction?

2. What daily acts of positivity can you cultivate in your life?

3. How do you currently express positivity to family members and friends?

4. What is one way you can use technology to express positivity, internally or to others?

5. What will you do today to express positivity to yourself or others?

Additional Resources

"Glass Half Full: Four Reasons Why It's Good to Be Optimistic," Kate Whiting, December 12, 2016. tinyurl.com/ycareyay

"Is Your Glass Half Empty or Half Full?" *Psychology Today.* Jennifer Kunst, March 14, 2012. tinyurl.com/y9chgglg

"Psychological Stress and Social Media Use," Keith Hampton, Lee Rainie, Weixu Lu, Inyoung Shin, & Kristen Purcell, January 15, 2015. pewinternet.org/2015/01/15/psychological-stress-and-social-media-use-2

"A Richer Life by Seeing the Glass Half Full," *The New York Times,* Jane E. Brody, May 21, 2012. well.blogs.nytimes.com/2012/05/21/a-richer-life-by-seeing-the-glass-half-full

"What You Need to Know Before Choosing Online Therapy," American Psychological Association. apa.org/helpcenter/online-therapy.aspx

"You Asked: Is Social Media Making Me Miserable?" *TIME,* Markham Heid. tinyurl.com/ycuam59j

ISTE Standards Connection

ISTE Standards for Educators 3a: Create experiences for learners to make positive, socially responsible contributions and exhibit empathetic behavior online that build relationships and community.

ISTE Standards for Educators 6d: Model and nurture creativity and creative expression to communicate ideas, knowledge, or connections.

ISTE Standards for Education Leaders 1d: Cultivate responsible online behavior, including the safe, ethical, and legal use of technology.

ISTE Standards for Education Leaders 5c: Use technology to regularly engage in reflective practices that support personal and professional growth.

Social media and other forms of online communication and collaboration can be leveraged to enhance relationships when users are challenged to think about how and why they use these platforms. Educators, and others who work with children, are uniquely positioned to model using various technologies in ways that lead to positive outcomes.

3

Getting Focused

We've all done it at one time or another. It's a weekday morning. You wake up late, take a quick shower, and waste precious time sorting out what to wear for an important meeting happening that afternoon. By the time you've gathered up the things you need to take to work, grabbed something to eat on the way and a cup of coffee, you probably won't make it to work on time. You get in your car, start the engine, and are off. You drive a little too fast, trying to make up lost time. Perhaps you take your eyes off the road briefly as you reach for your coffee cup or the breakfast you brought to eat while driving. Then your phone rings. Of course you wouldn't take a call while driving, but the ringtone is muffled and coming from somewhere near your feet. Now you're focused on figuring out how to retrieve the phone instead of minding the traffic. You make it to work with no time to spare, and suddenly realize you have little or no recollection of how you got there. Distracted driving is a very dangerous behavior, and it's just one example of how easily our focus is interrupted throughout the day. Whether it's allowing our minds to wander during a meeting or losing track of a conversation because of a nearby distraction, we spend much of our time unfocused.

Overview

Do you remember the first time you were told to quit daydreaming and pay attention? Probably not, although we would venture a guess you were very young. Our culture values attending to business over permitting the mind to wander. In fact, our stereotype of daydreamers is that they are lazy and unable to direct their attention to important matters. In a nation of "doers," daydreamers are considered slackers. In reality, everyone's mind wanders—as much as 50% of people's waking time is spent daydreaming. Contrary to popular thinking, there are many benefits to that state of mind (Frank, n.d.). So why are we including a chapter on the importance of getting focused? It is because there is a difference between allowing your mind to wander and being distracted. We would like readers to learn more about the benefits of mind-wandering while recognizing those times when being preoccupied becomes a drawback.

According to Jill Suttie, PsyD, "Mind-wandering seems to involve the default network of the brain, which is known to be active when we are not engaged directly in tasks and is also related to creativity" (2018). Thomas Cottle, an American sociologist and psychologist says, "Distraction means to divert or draw the mind away from something." But he says, "...the word *distraction* also means 'to cause conflict and confusion.'" (Cottle, 1993). While we recognize that not

---

WHERE TO FIND RESOURCES ON GETTING FOCUSED

Interested in learning more about daydreaming, distractions, and getting focused? Check out these articles on the web:

- **"What Does the Way Your Mind Wanders Reveal about You?"** (tinyurl.com/y84hwxjr): This article challenges the notion that a wandering mind is an unhappy mind.

- **"Easily Distracted: Why It's Hard to Focus and What to Do About It"** (tinyurl.com/y92zsb9u): What are some of the reasons we have difficulty focusing when we need to, and what can we do to avoid unproductive distractions?

- **"Strategies for Getting and Keeping the Brain's Attention"** (tinyurl.com/y8lxax5v): Strategies educators can use to help students recognize when they are losing their focus, and what they can do about it.

all daydreaming is positive, nor all distractions negative, for purposes of discussion in this chapter, we are going to use these two terms to differentiate between mind-wandering that is positive in nature (day-dreaming) and mind-wandering that tends to be negative (distraction). This will help further the discussion about when it is acceptable to lose focus, and when it is important to regain focus.

The Upside of Daydreaming

HAHA - Had to read this twice because my mind started wandering

Decades of research show that a wandering mind negatively impacts one's reading comprehension. There is also evidence that daydreaming adversely affects attention spans and performance on intelligence tests. However, recent research indicates that a wandering mind can also play a critical role in creative problem solving and goal setting (MacDonald, 2016). Additional research concludes that educators cannot expect students to be able to pay attention to the task at hand all the time. In fact, the longer the lesson or activity, the more likely that students' minds will wander. This research suggests that educators need to learn strategies for helping students manage their attention. For example, it helps to recognize that when a person's mind wanders, what is actually happening is something called *dishabituation*, giving her mind a quick break that enables her to return to a task with renewed focus (Pachai et al., 2016). Mind-wandering is also a way to relieve boredom, which is particularly beneficial for those engaged in mind-numbing tasks or situations.

The Downside of Being Distracted

In addition to the negative impacts mentioned (reductions in reading comprehension, attention span, and scores on intelligence tests), there are other downsides to distraction. For example, a recent survey by Udemy for Business showed that 70% of survey participants reported feeling distracted at work for a variety of reasons, including open workspaces, talkative coworkers, and meetings that were more inter-ruptive than informational. This resulted in decreased job satisfaction, increased stress, and reduced productivity (Thibodeaux, 2018).

Distractions negatively impact student performance. Listening to music while studying may be helpful, but watching television or videos, gaming, or surfing the web interfere with learning. A study conducted in 2006 by Russell A. Poldrack, a psychology professor at the University of California, Los Angeles, showed that people typically employ two learning strategies, memorization or habituation. Each type of learning uses a different area of the brain. Memorization relies on rote learning of facts, while habituation requires repeating an action over and over until it becomes second nature (University of California – Los Angeles, 2006). An AP report on CBS News about this study suggests that there may be a connection to classroom learning. When students are distracted, habituation takes over as the primary learning strategy; distracted students may pick up some knowledge but not get enough context to understand how or why it is so (Stevenson, 2006).

The Real-World Connection

When we read articles about distractions at work and school or talk with people about this topic, we get the impression that distraction is viewed as a state of mind that can easily be compartmentalized if people try hard enough to get it under control. But it's not that simple. Many people appear to live distracted lives. Either they are not paying attention to what's happening around them, or their attention is pulled in so many different directions that they find it impossible to focus on practically anything. For example, they meet friends for dinner but spend the entire evening dealing with text messages related to work. They use hands-free calling to talk with people while they are driving. They attend a child's choir performance and sit at the back of the auditorium so the light from the screen of whatever device they are using to write a report doesn't disturb other audience members. They show up, but they certainly are not present. People can learn ways to better deal with distraction, but this requires conscious effort and isn't always easy to do (Flaxington, 2015).

In their book, *The Distracted Mind: Ancient Brains in a High-Tech World* (2016), Gazzaley and Rosen identify two broad sources of distraction: internal and external. Internal interruptions are those times when we allow our minds to wander, while external interruptions are caused by someone or something outside our immediate control. We decide where we direct our attention, but we are often overwhelmed by the sheer volume of daily interference. This often results in reduced quality of life. Distractions are a part of life—it is not possible to eradicate them entirely—but that does not mean it is impossible to deal with them more effectively.

Current literature lays a lot of blame for distracted living on advances in technology, both devices and the amount of information that bombards us every day. The following sections on Technology and Getting Focused and Activities offer information and strategies you can use to help you regain your focus.

Technology and Getting Focused

The multitasking myth is the quintessential example of how the improper use of technology negatively affects our attention spans. To be fair, the notion that people can juggle multiple tasks at the same time existed prior to the digital age. As a single working parent with two small children, Susan spent years attempting to keep three, four, or more balls in the air with widely varying degrees of success (she never came close to doing this effectively). Fortunately for her, the children were in high school before cell phones first became available. As difficult as it was to multitask back then, advances in various technologies have upped the ante considerably. The hard truth is that our brains are not wired to deal with two or more unrelated tasks at the same time (Rosen and Samuel, 2015). What we think of as "multitasking" is more aptly described as serial interruption. Don't believe it? Here's a simple test: Try to read a page in a book while simultaneously carrying on a meaningful conversation with someone about a topic completely unrelated to your reading. It's simply not possible, yet many people attempt the equivalent of this every day.

The next time you are out and about, take a careful look around. No matter where you are or what you are doing, there is an excellent chance you'll see someone checking email or social media while making a purchase at a cash register, or taking a phone call while simultaneously attempting to follow a conversation with friends. You can observe similar behaviors in classrooms, libraries, offices—anywhere people have access to technology: A student regularly interrupting her work on a writing assignment to check Instagram; a library patron listening to a podcast while attempting to read a book; an office worker with many windows open on his laptop, struggling to find the one he needs for a report he is creating while conducting a meeting with a client. The result of trying to split our focus between two (or more) tasks is less efficiency—no task gets the attention it requires.

We tend to think we can handle routine, frequent interruptions by multitasking as well. Some of these interruptions are self-imposed, but others come from coworkers, colleagues, family members, and friends. Email, texts, online messaging services, social media posts, and phone calls all demand our attention. We tell ourselves it takes little time to respond to the demands of others, but when an interruption requires you to shift gears from one topic to another, it can take as long as 23 minutes to refocus on what you were doing prior to the interruption (Mark, 2008).

Multitasking also takes a physical toll on you. When you try to juggle important tasks, your body responds by releasing adrenaline and stress hormones that cause an energy rush. This increased drive does not help you to complete tasks more quickly or efficiently. Instead, prolonged high levels of stress lead to headaches, stomachaches, sleep interruption, and other physical symptoms. In addition, the quality of your work suffers when you attempt to multitask. People who are interrupted frequently do not have opportunities to think deeply about what they are doing. Shallow thinking results in short-term memory loss. This means you need to repeat your work because you cannot remember what you were doing when the interruption happened.

That said, not all interruptions are bad. For example, quick breaks to clear your head (e.g., taking a short walk or a few minutes of deep breathing) can allow you to bring yourself back to a task with renewed focus. Pausing briefly to answer a question from someone who is working on a task related to what you are doing is also less disruptive. This is because it is easier to get back to what you were doing when interrupted if you have not had to shift your thinking to an entirely different topic.

So, what strategies can you use to avoid interruptions and stay focused? When it comes to technology use, it may be as much a case of what *not* to do with the technology as what to do with it. Here are a few suggestions.

1. **Avoid technology-induced sleep disruption.** Many people use their smartphones as alarm clocks. It makes sense, but once the phone is in their bedrooms, it is a small leap from alarm clock to distraction. The temptation to check email, texts, and social media before falling asleep, if you wake up during the night, or first

thing in the morning is a huge sleep disruptor. Technology-free late-evening and early-morning routines help you fall asleep more quickly, sleep more soundly, and start a new day with fewer distractions.

2. **Turn off all message notifications on your devices.** Aural and visual notifications of new messages cause interruptions throughout your day. Hearing that chime or seeing that text bubble distracts you, even if you do not check the new message. A better approach is to schedule a couple of times during the day to read and respond to new messages. This may be difficult initially because you have probably trained people that you reply to messages quickly. However, given a little time and patience, it is possible to change people's expectations. Of course, you will have certain people to whom you will always respond immediately, but set distinctive notifications so you are interrupted only when absolutely necessary.

3. **Schedule breaks.** If you spend a lot of time at a desk or using a computer, you probably forget to get up and move around throughout the day. There are apps and web-based tools you can download to set up break times. For example, TomatoTimer (tomato-timer.com) is a web-based tool that reminds you to take a 5-minute break every 25 minutes and a 10-minute break about every hour. Another option is the Eye Care 20 20 20 app (iOS and Android) which reminds you to give your eyes a short break every 20 minutes. You can also use the task scheduler built into your computer's operating system for this purpose.

4. **Block access to distractors.** Some folks are so habituated to checking social media throughout the day that they need additional assistance to limit this behavior. There are browser extensions (e.g., StayFocusd or WasteNoTime) and apps (SelfControl or OffTime) you can use to temporarily block access to social media for periods of time you specify.

5. **To-do lists.** An old-fashioned daily to-do list can help you keep your focus. There are a number of apps and other online tools you can use to create lists, such as Wunderlist, Trello, or Things. Or your web-based calendar may include a task feature that can be used for the same purpose. The important thing about lists is that you make them realistic (How much can you really accomplish

in a day?) and prioritized so you tackle the most important items during those times you can be most productive.

Technology does not cause us to multitask. However, thoughtful use of devices can help us avoid serial interruption, which causes us to lose our focus.

Activities

Here are eight activities you can use to refocus your attention when you find yourself distracted. Six are individual and can be done almost anywhere; two require working with a partner. Kids enjoy all of these activities. The sidebar includes web resources that can be used to enhance activities 1 and 2.

1. **Relaxing breathing:** This activity may be done lying, sitting, or standing. If lying, place your arms at your sides, palms facing upward. If sitting or standing, have both feet flat on the floor, arms at your sides. Breathe deeply, down into your belly. It may help to count of five as you inhale through your nose. Then immediately exhale through your mouth to the count to five. Do this for three to five minutes. How did you feel before you started this exercise? How do you feel now? If possible, do this exercise once daily. It will relieve stress and help you get focused.

2. **Coloring:** You have probably heard about the adult coloring-book craze. Although coloring books for adults have been around for a long time, recent interest in the connection between coloring and focus is likely an underlying reason for their current popularity. You need: a little time; crayons, markers, or colored pencils (inexpensive sets range in size from 8 to 100 or more colors); and a coloring book or plain paper to create your own designs. Many people find that coloring is a relaxing experience because you focus on the task at hand and not on sources of stress. Take a break and give it a try; see what you can create.

3. **Three deep breaths:** The next time you are feeling impatient, anxious, or angry, take three deep breaths. Stop, exhale completely, inhale fully (make your abdomen rise), and exhale completely. Repeat until you have taken three deep breaths. How do you feel? Taking time to breathe allows you to distance yourself from

Activity ❶   RELAXING BREATHING: Online Tools

Once you see the benefits of simple breathing exercises, you may decide to explore short meditations designed to help you focus on your breathing. An easy way to get started is to explore guided meditations available on YouTube. Because they are free, the quality does vary widely, but by taking the time to explore what's available, you will find some that work for you. There are also apps for iOS and Android devices that offer guided meditations. Check the appropriate app store to find them.

Activity ❷   COLORING: Online Tools

Interested in giving coloring a try, but not feeling terribly creative? There are hundreds of free adult coloring sheets available online, just waiting for you to download. Here are two:

- **Faber-Castell** (fabercastell.com/art-and-graphic/adult-coloring-books/coloring-pages-for-adults): Faber-Castell promotes opportunities for people to experience creativity throughout their lifetimes. They offer a line of coloring books for adults, and there are currently more than 25 free coloring sheets available on their website for downloading.

- **Just Color** (justcolor.net): This website offers more than 1500 free coloring pages for adults organized into six different galleries. Coloring pages for kids are also available.

most situations. Your level of anxiety, anger, or impatience will decrease with each breath. Now that you have had a moment to collect yourself, you can deal with the challenge or problem facing you. And the best part is you can employ this strategy anywhere, anytime.

4. **Flower and candle:** Breathing is such an unconscious activity, we rarely pay attention to it. But when we do, we reap some substantial benefits. Focusing on the act of breathing resets our thinking and feelings in many situations. Taking a conscious breath or two brings us back to ourselves and the miracle of life—breathing in and breathing out. Here is an idea for a visual aid that can remind you to breathe and also be used to encourage deep breathing. You will need an unlined three-by-five-inch index card and two

pictures: one of a flower in bloom, and one of a burning candle. (Select images that will fit on the card, one on each side.) Glue or tape the picture of the flower on one side and the burning candle on the other. If you cannot find images you like, draw your own. Whenever you want or need to breathe, hold the index card in your hand and look at the flower. Take a deep breath, as if you are smelling the blossom. Hold that breath for a moment, then turn the card over and blow out the candle, with a breath that is a little longer than the breath you took in. Repeat a couple of times. Keep the index card in a prominent place, perhaps on your desk, so you have a visual reminder to pause and breathe.

5. **Take a walk:** Next time you are feeling overwhelmed or pulled in too many directions, stop what you are doing and take a walk. Whether you have five minutes to spare or an hour, taking a walk is an excellent way to break out of a rut and get re-centered. You do not need anything special to get up and get outdoors. If possible, let your mind wander as you take your stroll. For those times when negative thoughts overwhelm you, try listening to bright music or a guided meditation as you walk. You should return to whatever you were doing feeling refreshed and focused. You may find it helpful to build a short walk into your daily routine. Fifteen or twenty minutes of walking after lunch, or in lieu of a coffee break, can make a difference in your sense of well-being. Give it a try.

6. **Blowing bubbles:** Taking time out to focus on your breathing can be done in a multitude of ways. Did you enjoy blowing bubbles as a child? As an adult, you can use them as an aid for breathing. All you need is a bottle of bubble solution, a wand, and an outdoor space where you don't need to worry about spills. As you blow, experiment with ways to control the size of the bubbles by altering your breathing pattern. To take your bubble-blowing experience up a notch, accompany the activity with a YouTube version of "I'm Forever Blowing Bubbles," such as one sung by Doris Day (youtube.com/watch?v=H6SXi4I47Qw).

7. **What's different?** Have you noticed how easy it is to pay little or no attention to the people, places, and things around you? This is particularly true when you have a lot on your mind. Instead of focusing, our minds flit from one thing to the next. Nothing gets serious consideration. This partner activity is designed to

help you pay more attention to things right in front of your face. One person is the observer, and the other person is the observed. Stand facing one another. The observer looks at the observed for one minute, mentally noting as much as possible about the person's appearance (clothing, accessories, hairstyle, etc.). After one minute, the partners turn their backs to one another for 30 seconds. During this time, the observed changes one thing about his or her appearance. The partners face one another again, and the observer has 30 seconds to identify what is different. Change roles and repeat. What happened? As observer, were you able to identify the change? How difficult was it to see the change? What does this tell you about your own powers of perception?

8. **Mirror image:** In this activity, partners work together and take turns leading. One person is the leader, and the other is the mirror. The point is to encourage careful observation and concentration. Initially staying with upper body movements, the leader moves and the mirror partner tries to follow exactly, but in "reverse" (as if looking in a mirror). The leader is not trying to trick the mirror, so smooth movements are more easily followed than sudden, abrupt ones. After a time, the partners shift roles. It is possible to switch partners midstream to practice smooth transitions. We encourage people to look into their partner's eyes rather than trying to follow their hands or arms. That way, they can build up their concentration as well as an awareness of movement through peripheral vision.

Questions for Reflection

1. What role does daydreaming play in your sense of life satisfaction? When does achieving a sense of life satisfaction require you to resist distractions?

2. What daily acts can you cultivate in your life that will help you focus when necessary?

3. How do you currently dodge daydreaming or distraction when you are with family members and friends?

4. What is one strategy you can use to avoid using technology as a distraction? What are ways you can use technology to support creative thinking?

5. What will you do today to curtail distractions at appropriate times?

Additional Resources

"Are You Grounded? Centered? Or Both?" *Psychology Today,* Diana Raab, May 23, 2017. tinyurl.com/ycx6csxh

"Attention Please," *TED Radio Hour,* May 25, 2018. npr.org/programs/ted-radio-hour/614007696/attention-please

"Five Reasons We Multitask Anyway," *Psychology Today,* Joanne Cantor, May 31, 2010. tinyurl.com/yc5rmppn

"Focus on the Moment," *Magazine of the Society of Women Engineers, 60*(1), Catherine Rocky, 2014. sites.uci.edu/mindfulhs/files/2014/04/Focus-on-the-Moment.pdf

"How to Focus a Wandering Mind," *Daily Good,* Wendy Hasenkamp, April 18, 2015. tinyurl.com/l59h3gh

"Multitasking and stress," *HealthDay,* Chris Woolston, January 20, 2018. tinyurl.com/y8awpclv

"New Study Shows Humans Are on Autopilot Nearly Half the Time," *Psychology Today,* David Rock, November 14, 2010. tinyurl.com/ydhlouv3

"The Perils of Multitasking," *Psychology Today,* William R. Klemm, August 26, 2016. tinyurl.com/y9e9s8ng

"Remedies for the Distracted Mind," *Behavioral Scientist,* Adam Gazzaley & Larry D. Rosen, January 8, 2018. behavioralscientist.org/remedies-distracted-mind

"A Wandering Mind Isn't Just a Distraction: It May Be Your Brain's Default State," *HuffPost,* Carolyn Gregoire, November 4, 2016. tinyurl.com/y92d7av3

"What Are Everyday Daydreamers Like?" *Scientific American,* Scott Barry Kaufman, March 20, 2017. tinyurl.com/kzvzuz8

"Why Daydreamers Are More Creative," *Psychology Today,* Scott Barry Kaufman, February 28, 2011. tinyurl.com/yccbpc8r

ISTE Standards Connection

ISTE Standards for Educators 1c: Stay current with research that supports improved student learning outcomes, including findings from the learning sciences.

ISTE Standards for Education Leaders 2a: Engage education stakeholders in developing and adopting a shared vision for using technology to improve student success, informed by the learning sciences.

ISTE Standards for Education Leaders 5a: Set goals to remain current on emerging technologies for learning, innovations in pedagogy and advancements in the learning sciences.

Digital devices do not have to lead to serial interruptions that cause us to lose our focus, but adults and kids must learn ways to use these technologies thoughtfully. When educators and others who work with children understand that digital tools are designed to keep users coming back, and understand how those features impact learning, they are able to create environments in which technology supports learning.

4

Empathy

🖎 *In a recent workshop* on differentiated instruction sponsored by Saint Mary's College as part of their Distinguished Speaker Series, Dr. Carol Ann Tomlinson related an incident that took place in one of her schools. It was a place in which children came and left frequently, and many, many languages were spoken (by the children, not necessarily by the staff). A small group of children would get together when a new child came into the room, surround the child, and wait for him or her to speak. When that happened, they would escort the child around the room, meeting other students, until they found someone who spoke the new child's language. Then they could leave the newcomer with their new friend who could orient the new child to the classroom in a familiar language.

Overview

Empathy lies at the core of what it means to be human. Without empathy, we feel disconnected from other people and struggle to confirm our own place in the human family. Being able to empathize is critical, especially in a world where there are so many people with so many different ideas. If we can take a moment to consider other viewpoints, our own become clearer—and are perhaps enriched by ideas that had not occurred to us.

According to Psychology Today's website, "Empathy is the experience of understanding another person's thoughts, feelings, and condition from their point of view, rather than from your own. You can imagine yourself in their place in order to understand what they are feeling or experiencing." A similar definition can be found at the *Greater Good Magazine* site: "Empathy is the ability to sense other people's emotions, coupled with the ability to imagine what someone else might be thinking or feeling." Paul Ekman (2010) defines three kinds of empathy—cognitive, emotional, and compassionate. Cognitive empathy is simply understanding another's feelings. Emotional empathy is described by Daniel Goleman (2010) as "when you physically feel what other people feel, as though their emotions were contagious." Compassionate empathy extends emotional empathy to the point where one feels he or she must respond and act.

C. Daniel Batson (2009) expands the idea even further. He says, "The term *empathy* is currently applied to more than a half-dozen phenomena" (p. 1). They include conceiving what another is thinking and feeling on a deep level, "feeling distress at witnessing another person's suffering" (p. 7).

It is heartening to see that many people are exploring empathy and its importance in our daily lives. As social beings, we depend on one another for many things. Without people we trust and care about, our lives would be diminished. We hope you will find information and activities here to enhance yours.

The Real-World Connection

Why is empathy important to, and good for, us? Research suggests empathic people tend to be more generous and concerned with others' welfare, and they also tend to have happier relationships and greater personal well-being. Empathy can also improve leadership ability and facilitate effective communication ("Empathy Quiz," 2018).

Indeed, "To effectively navigate the social world, it is important to understand others, infer their thoughts and feelings, and to effectively connect to their emotional experiences. Put differently, the extent to which one can empathize with others is a key component of a successful social interaction" (Olderbak, Sassenrath, Keller, & Wilhelm, 2014).

Brené Brown distinguishes between sympathy and empathy in her research, which finds that the importance of building connections outweighs our fight or flight responses. Authentic connections are built on empathy, in which people do the work required to understand one another through shared experiences, rather than simply offering advice (even if that advice comes from a place of caring). She says, "Empathy fuels connection; sympathy drives disconnection.

WHERE TO FIND RESOURCES ON EMPATHY

Take a look at these sites to further your understanding of the value of empathy in daily life.

- **Greater Good Website: Empathy** (greatergood.berkeley.edu/empathy): Out of the Greater Good Science Center at the University of California, Berkeley, this website includes information and links to resources on a variety of topics related to well-being, including empathy.

- **Psychology Today Website: Empathy** (psychologytoday.com/basics/empathy): This website includes three main sections: All About Empathy, Recent Posts on Empathy, and Empathy Essential Reads.

- **Start Empathy Website** (startempathy.org): You might want to begin with the Start Empathy Toolkit (startempathy.org/resources/toolkit), and then explore other articles and resources.

Rarely can a response make something better. What makes something better is connection" (The RSA, 2013).

EMPATHY TRAINING

In her TEDx talk, Dr. Helen Riess explains that "every human being has a longing to be seen, understood, and appreciated." To that end, she has developed training for medical students and others, using the acronym EMPATHY to remind us what to observe (EMPATH), and the importance of our response based on those observations (Y).

E—*Eye contact*

M—*Muscles of facial expression*

P—*Posture*

A—*Affect*

T—*Tone of voice*

H—*Hearing the whole person*

Y—*Your response*

For a full explanation, see Dr. Riess' TEDx Talk at https://www.youtube.com/watch?v=baHrcC8B4WM

In Roman Krznaric's article (2012), he cites a shift in the study of how we understand human nature to consider ourselves as "*homo empathicus*, wired for empathy, social cooperation, and mutual aid." This is good news! We can improve our empathy skills by taking a look at the six habits that empathic people have cultivated.

1. **Habit 1:** Cultivate curiosity about strangers. Wherever they go, empathic people seek to understand those around them. They engage strangers in conversation to better know what the other is thinking. Krznaric says, "Set yourself the challenge of having a conversation with one stranger every week. All it requires is courage" (2012).

2. **Habit 2:** Challenge prejudices and discover commonalities. Looking for common ground rather than holding on to only our own worldviews allows for deeper understanding of ourselves, and of those with different viewpoints.

3. **Habit 3:** Try another person's life. It is fairly easy to listen with empathy to another's views, but the harder road is to challenge oneself to step out of our comfort zone and visit another religion's church, or (similar to the king who donned peasant's clothes and walked among his people to get a firsthand view of their thoughts on his governing) put ourselves in the actual position of the person we are trying to understand.

4. **Habit 4:** Listen hard and open up. Actively listen—be present and carefully attend to what another person is saying without jumping in with your own thoughts or experiences. A vital part of listening, according to Krznaric, is responding in an empathetic way by making oneself vulnerable: "Empathy is a two-way street. At its best, it is built upon mutual understanding—an exchange of our most important beliefs and experiences" (2012).

5. **Habit 5:** Inspire mass action and social change. When enough people share empathy toward a person or cause, changes can occur. One idea is to cultivate connection through social media to build empathy, and thus movement toward action and positive outcomes.

6. **Habit 6:** Develop an ambitious imagination. Pretend you are a member of a group or organization to which you are opposed. What does it feel like to look through their eyes? How might that understanding build a bridge for a conversation, an action step, or finding common ground? Initiatives such as Roots of Empathy (Gordon, 2011) and the Toolkit for Promoting Empathy (Borowsky, 2015) suggest ways to help students grow their empathy. As adults who model empathy, we are the most powerful advocates for its practice.

According to Krznaric, "The 20th century was the Age of Introspection, when self-help and therapy culture encouraged us to believe that the best way to understand who we are and how to live was to look inside ourselves. But it left us gazing at our own navels. The 21st century should become the Age of Empathy, when we discover ourselves not simply through self-reflection, but by becoming interested in the lives of others. We need empathy to create a new kind of revolution. Not an old-fashioned revolution built on new laws, institutions, or policies, but a radical revolution in human relationships" (2012).

We have opportunities all around us to pay attention to Krznaric's observation. For self-care, for well-being, for a better world locally and globally, building empathy offers paths to understanding and cooperation in a fractured world.

Technology and Empathy

You may have heard of cyber vigilantism—the use of online tools to take the law into one's own hands through virtual means. The term *digilante* has been coined to refer to someone who engages in this behavior. Well-known examples include groups such as Wikileaks and Anonymous, as well as individuals such as Edward Snowden, Chelsea Manning, and Julian Assange. These people and groups have taken it upon themselves to find and release information that makes confidential (and often illegal) activities public. Regardless of whether you think their actions are acceptable, they have circumvented societal systems intended to protect people and institutions.

An increasingly common form of cyber vigilantism is online shaming. Supporters claim online shaming brings people to justice, but more often than not, innocent people suffer or the consequences meted out far exceed the supposed transgression. For example, in August of 2017, Kyle Quinn, an assistant professor at the University of Arkansas was enjoying a quiet evening with his wife. Unbeknownst to him, a group of white supremacists were gathering in Charlottesville, Virginia. Photos of this group were posted online, and someone identified one of the participants as Kyle Quinn. In very short order, people who did not know him were shaming Quinn on social media sites, sending aggressive messages to his work email, and leaving threatening messages on his work voicemail. The actual person in the photo was later identified, but by that time, Quinn and his wife feared for their personal safety (Pogue, 2017).

Ready access makes it easy for people to shame one another online. Most people carry mobile devices capable of snapping photos or recording videos that are easily uploaded to social media sites. In the past we might have observed inappropriate behavior, pointed it out to the friend walking next to us, and kept going on our way. Now we can document the behavior and share it with millions of people in seconds—people who may decide the person's behavior warrants some kind of punishment.

Another factor is something called the "toxic disinhibition effect," which describes how people are willing to say and do things online they would never do in real life, such as shame someone they do not know or engage in other mob-like behaviors (Suler, 2004). Educators and students often have a very strong sense of right and wrong or fairness. This quality is often benign, but under the right circumstances, it can lead them to engage in online shaming. As a result, it is important for members of the school community to be aware of, and guard against, the temptation to participate in online shaming.

Because it is so easy to ruin someone's reputation by spreading lies, a call for empathy can curtail a disastrous situation. Applying common sense, placing ourselves in another's shoes, and asking if it helps the common good to forward hurtful stories will help build our own habits of empathy and ultimately make the world a safer, kinder place.

A number of websites provide starting places for exploring personal empathy. Take *Greater Good Magazine*'s Empathy Quiz, in which you are presented with a series of statements and indicate how much (or little) they apply to you. At the end, you are given a score, along with some suggestions for improving empathy, such as "practice active listening," "share in other people's joy," "look for commonalities with others," "read fiction," and "pay attention to faces."

Another online resource is the Reading the Mind in the Eyes test. Created by Professor Simon Baron-Cohen, director of the Autism Research Centre at the University of Cambridge, initially to identify autism, the online version of the test provides you with the opportunity to choose the emotion a person is feeling by viewing only their eyes in a series of photographs. At the end, you are given a score that can be compared to scores of people who are considered good at reading others' emotions. You can take the test online: questionwritertracker.com/quiz/61/Z4MK3TKB.html.

Paul Ekman's work on micro-expressions (2018) can help us consider our impressions of others with as little information as is given through their eyes. Learning online about the quick assumptions we make about other people in an online test can help us pause a moment as we consider our encounters with others in daily life.

Kathleen Morris (2018) suggests that creating opportunities for students to blog builds empathy. We can take her advice as adults, and build relationships through blogging with colleagues and like-minded people throughout the world. Her "netiquette" points apply to all of us. While blogging:

1. give compliments

2. deliver feedback constructively

3. ask questions and engage in conversation

4. be a reliable online friend

5. stay relevant and on-topic

6. avoid ambiguous communication (e.g., ALL CAPS could be interpreted as shouting)

Building and enhancing our own empathic abilities are crucial to living a meaningful and connected life. Rebecca Detrick (2017) sums it up: "An adult who understands that by building human connections and being open to understanding the experiences of others, a person's life will be richer, their support systems expansive, and their goals broader and achievable" (p. 7).

Activities

Here are several activities that help focus on empathy. The idea is to clarify your own thoughts on a topic while considering other points of view. Six of these activities are individual; two will work with more than one person. The first seven of these can be adapted for a variety of situations in which children work in pairs or small groups, while the eighth activity can be interesting in a whole-group setting.

1. **Find common ground:** One way to explore another's viewpoint is to invite a friend, colleague, or family member to share a discussion with you. Together, pick a topic you are both interested in exploring. It could be a personal issue, or a topic in the news. Each person writes down his or her thoughts about the topic and shares their thoughts, which allows both parties to see patterns and common areas of concern or interest. Online collaboration tools allow for sharing ideas asynchronously.

2. **Walk in someone's shoes, part 1:** Recall an incident in which someone did or said something that you did not understand. In your journal, write your response to the incident and your

Activity ❶   FINDING COMMON GROUND:
Online Tools

- **Online collaboration tools:** Google Docs (docs.google.com) and Microsoft 365 (office.com) offer settings where you can create a file and share it with others. Perhaps you want to have a conversation with a colleague about a new activity idea that is very different from what has been done previously, but there is not time to get together in person. Create an online file and share it with your colleague! You can both enter your thoughts; consider dating each entry so you can see how the conversation evolves. Entries can be color-coded for easy identification of the writer. Hopefully, this exchange will not take the place of a face-to-face discussion, if that is feasible. However, it can provide a space where thinking and consideration can take place to lay the foundation for an in-person conversation. It also provides an opportunity for both parties to see where their thoughts meet and where there is a disconnection.

- **Online collaboration tools:** Mind Mapping is one way to organize your thoughts and create a visual representation of them. Both MindMeister (mindmeister.com) and Coggle (coggle.it) offer free options for creating mind maps, and both allow for building mind maps collaboratively.

Activity ❷   WALK IN SOMEONE'S SHOES:
Online Tools

- **Traditional tales retold:** By reading and thinking about traditional stories, we build empathy. Stories create a bridge between the teller or writer and the listener or reader. Research some of your favorite stories to find variations from different parts of the world, and write your thoughts about the differences; focus on how empathetic (or not) a particular character feels in the different versions. Share your thoughts with a friend or colleague, through social media, Google Docs, or other formats.

- **Digital personal expression:** At StoryCenter (storycenter.org), you can create a digital story using your voice, images, music, and other effects. My Hero Project (myhero.com) features written stories, short films, and artwork created by children and adults from around the world. Contributing to sites such as these, as well as viewing the contributions, can lead to interesting discussions and deeper understanding of the creators and their subjects.

assumptions about it. After you have finished, consider the possible point of view of someone else in the incident. Retell the story in your journal from the other person's point of view.

3. **Walk in someone's shoes, part 2:** Retell or rewrite in your journal a familiar folk or fairy tale from the perspective of a character other than the traditional one. For example, "The Three Billy Goats Gruff" could be told from the point of view of the troll, the bridge, or the grass.

4. **Dilemma stories, part 1:** Dilemma stories are those in which there are a number of possible outcomes. Read "The Cow-tail Switch" (available online at westafrikanoralliterature.weebly.com/the-cow-tail-switch.html). Think about which son should be given the cow-tail switch; share your reasons in your journal, or with a partner. Challenge yourself to consider another recipient—what reasons might another son be given the prize?

5. **Dilemma stories, part 2:** "Jack and the Beanstalk" is a familiar tale. Tell, listen to, or read the story. Then think about Jack on a continuum. Is he a hero or a villain? Where would you place him? Share reasons for your position in your journal.

6. **Listen to me!:** In this activity, a pair works together. One person has 30 seconds to tell the story of a personal incident that happened recently. Then the listener has 60 seconds to retell the same story *as if it happened to them,* (i.e., in the first person). The pair talks about what difference it made for the listener to have more time to tell the story, then they switch roles.

7. **Telephone:** This traditional activity still teaches the value of listening carefully to build empathy. A group of people stands in a circle, and one person whispers a message to the person next to her. That person then repeats the same message to the next person, and so on, until the message has gone all the way around the circle. Inevitably, the final message is totally different from the one that was started, or at the very least, is a garbled version of it. The group splits into partners and talks about why they think the message changed. How does empathy between teller and listener factor into what is heard and conveyed? What precautions can we take to make sure our own messages are accurately heard and understood?

8. **Were you ever:** Consider this activity for a staff meeting. Designate a "yes" side of the room and a "no" side. Suggest a series of questions and have people stand on one side of the room or the other, based on whether they have experienced the situation (e.g., Were you ever denied employment because of your gender?). Talk with others on your side of the room. Continue asking questions. If yes, move to the other side of the room; if no, stay put. Talk with others near you. You might conclude the series with the questions: Have you ever seen a situation where someone was discriminated against because of their age? and Have you been asked to intervene in such a situation? Share experiences.

Questions for Reflection

1. Why do you think empathy is an important skill to cultivate?

2. How can you increase the practice of empathy?

3. Is it easier to be empathetic to friends or family? Why?

4. What is one way you can use technology to foster empathy?

5. What will you do today to increase empathy in your life?

Additional Resources

"Are We Entering an Age of Empathy?" *Neuro Research Project: NeuroNotes*, Ray Williams, March, 2012. neuroresearchproject.com/2012/03/14/greed-is-out-empathy-is-in

"Building Blocks for Digital Citizenship" [Cyber Vigilantism tab], Susan Brooks-Young & Dan Morris. livebinders.com/play/play?id=53885&backurl=/shelf/my

"The Classroom Versus the Computer: Or, Can You Learn Communication Skills behind a Screen?" Marie Bryson, January 18, 2018. tinyurl.com/y9v6un9v

Factitious [online game], Jolt & AU Game Lab, 2018. factitious.augamestudio.com

"Micro Expressions," Paul Ekman Group, 2018. paulekman.com/resources/micro-expressions

The Power of Empathy: Helen Riess at TEDxMiddlebury, Helen Riess, December 12, 2013. youtube.com/watch?v=baHrcC8B4WM&t=2s

"The Power of Vulnerability," Brené Brown, June, 2010. ted.com/talks/brene_brown_on_vulnerability

"Reading the Mind in the Eyes Test," 2009. questionwritertracker.com/quiz/61/Z4MK3TKB.html

"The 'Reading the Mind in the Eyes' Test Revised Version: A Study with Normal Adults, and Adults with Asperger Syndrome or High-Functioning Austim," *Journal of Child Psychology*, 42(2), Simon Baron-Cohen, Sally Wheelwright, Jacqueline Hill, Yogini Raste, & Ian Plumb, 2001. tinyurl.com/yc48vd8v

"To Test Your Fake News Judgment, Play This Game," *NPR*, Tennessee Watson, July 3, 2017. tinyurl.com/ybzqhbea

ISTE Standards Connection

ISTE Standards for Educators 1c: Stay current with research that supports improved student learning outcomes, including findings from the learning sciences.

ISTE Standards for Educators 3a: Create experiences for learners to make positive, socially responsible contributions and exhibit empathetic behavior online that build relationships and community.

ISTE Standards for Educators 5a: Use technology to create, adapt, and personalize learning experiences that foster independent learning and accommodate learner differences and needs.

ISTE Standards for Education Leaders 3d: Support educators in using technology to advance learning that meets the diverse learning, cultural, and social-emotional needs of individual students.

ISTE Standards for Education Leaders 5b: Participate regularly in online learning networks to collaboratively learn with and mentor other professionals.

Teachers, and others who work with children, can model their own online collaborative practices, as well as exhibit empathy in face-to-face and online interactions with kids. Empathy toward colleagues, in mentoring relationships, and with children allows the creation of authentic and caring learning environments.

5

Kindness

In Dr. Helen Riess's TEDx Talk (2013), she describes an incident she observed while traveling by air. As often happens with air travel, she found herself with a screaming child nearby. Try as the mother might, she could not quiet her child. Dr. Riess noticed a small child climb down from her seat, walk over to the crying child, and offer her own pacifier. Even very small children can see when someone is in distress and offer an act of kindness.

Overview

For those of us of a certain age, the epitome of kindness is Fred Rogers, whose *Mr. Rogers' Neighborhood* television series invariably portrayed care and respect for everyone, and always recognized each person's goodness. By being kind to others, Mr. Rogers demonstrated, life was happier for everyone involved. We love his famous quote:

"There are three ways to ultimate success: The first way is to be kind. The second way is to be kind. The third way is to be kind" (Bryson, 2018).

WHERE TO FIND RESOURCES ON KINDNESS

For more information on the value of kindness, we suggest these resources:

- **Center for Healthy Minds,** University of Wisconsin–Madison (centerhealthyminds.org): The Center offers a free kindness curriculum, as well as articles and research on kindness in a variety of settings.

- **Playful Learning,** Resources for Teaching Kindness (playfullearning.net/resource/resources-teaching-kindness): At this delightful website, you will find resources for teaching kindness through lessons in content areas as well as technology and engineering, global studies, well-being, and social-emotional learning. Additional resources include picture and chapter books, recommended products, and a subscription-based Teachers Lounge.

The Real-World Connection

Self-described self-centered New Yorkers Jessica Walsh and Tim Goodman decided to spend a year being kind. They came up with 12 different ways to do that and have shared their ideas on their website, 12 Kinds of Kindness. Their steps include smiling at everyone you meet, finding ways to "pay it forward," forgive and forget, and taking care not to beat yourself up. One intriguing idea was to put wallets with a little money in them around the city, with a note that asked the finder to do one kind thing with the cash.

You, too, can become a Random Acts of Kindness activist (RAKtivist)! Check out the Random Acts of Kindness website (randomactsofkindness.org), where research and lesson plans for students K–12 are available at no cost, and pledge to be kind to others. Indeed, "anyone who believes kindness can change the world, who reminds everyone around them how much love there is in the world, who inspires hope and generosity with their actions as much as their words—they are a RAKtivist." Simple acts such as opening the door for someone, offering to carry a package, and giving up a seat in a crowded venue count as kindnesses. The benefits to our own bodies and psyches are bountiful.

Psychotherapist Peter Field (2015) cites five reasons why kindness is important in our lives:

1. It is inbuilt—even very young children respond when they see someone who needs help.

2. It can have positive effects on the brain.

3. It can help you live longer.

4. It is contagious.

5. It makes you happier.

The Random Acts of Kindness website cites a variety of studies, including the work of Dr. David Hamilton (2017), to show that kindness offers many benefits, including increasing oxytocin. "Witnessing acts of kindness produces oxytocin, occasionally referred to as the 'love hormone' which aids in lowering blood pressure and improving our overall heart-health. Oxytocin also increases our self-esteem and optimism, which is extra helpful when we're anxious or shy in a social situation (randomactsofkindness.org/the-science-of-kindness). Kindness also increases energy, happiness, lifespan, pleasure, and serotonin, a natural healing, calming hormone. It decreases pain, stress, anxiety, depression, and blood pressure, according to the cited studies.

Self-Kindness

We all know the emergency instructions given on airplanes: In the case of lack of oxygen, masks will drop; adults should secure their own masks before helping children or others. It is the same with kindness. If you are not being kind to yourself, how can you be kind to others? When you feel positive about yourself, doing the same for others is easy, and it increases your own pleasure. There are many ways to be kind to yourself. The first step is to observe your own behavior and consider how you talk to yourself when you make a mistake, or something turns out differently than you had hoped. Do you hear compassionate self-talk, or is that inner voice chastising you? Do you speak to yourself as you speak to friends, or would you never say to a friend the things you say to yourself? See if you can decrease negative self-talk and substitute it with kinder messages. You get to write the story of your life and the inner dialogue that takes place within it.

According to Gregory L. Jantz (2016), founder of The Center and author of more than 30 books, "Positive self-talk is not self-deception. It is not mentally looking at circumstances with eyes that see only what you want to see. Rather, positive self-talk is about recognizing the truth, in situations and in yourself."

An infographic by Anna Vital, titled "How Not to Be Hard on Yourself," includes ideas such as "accept your weaknesses as your 'features'" and "surround yourself with people who want you to succeed." Perhaps by turning conventional wisdom on its head, we can start to see how much we learn from things that do not turn out as we expected, and instead take us in new, more meaningful directions.

In preparation for times when you make a mistake, create a list of the positive things you both are and do. When something does not go according to your plan (and it will—for all of us), see if you can recall your list and quiet any internal dialogues about past failures by turning the message around in a positive way for yourself. For example, "I can never do things right" could be transformed to, "I'm having difficulty right now, but I have already achieved so much." A commitment to becoming more self-compassionate makes life easier for all of us, as well as those around us. Let's work at treating ourselves as we would our best friends, and be kind to ourselves.

Forgiveness

Forgiving yourself and others can be a great act of kindness. Forgiveness allows one to move past anger and resentment, for example, which can become debilitating.

It is often more difficult to forgive ourselves than to forgive others. A major component of positive self-talk is to recognize that we all have shortcomings and accept them or figure out ways to change or overcome them. Blaming oneself is nonproductive and causes harm to our psyches.

Paul Dunion (2016) says, "Becoming more effective at self-forgiveness is simply a way to remain responsible for our self-worth. It is also a large welcome to our humanity as we release perfectionistic ambitions and attend to the task of inner reconciliation."

When we forgive ourselves, we can make new plans, we can move forward, we can act rather than feel hopeless and stymied. We found that Johanna Beyer's (2017) question cut to the heart of how we think about self-kindness: "If I asked you to name all the things that you love, how long would it take for you to name yourself?"

Technology and Kindness

Many opportunities abound for personal connections online. The internet affords us chances to meet people and share ideas, and offers occasions for both personal and private ventures. The downside of all these digital exchanges, in terms of kindness, is that we spend more time online than we do face-to-face with real people. The value of real-life friends and supporters cannot be underestimated. Family and friends help us define who we are in both the world and relationships. Positive exchanges build confidence and increase our ability to be compassionate and kind to others.

An obvious use of technology to further kindness in the world is participating in global exchanges among educators or classes. Projects such as Global Schoolhouse (globalschoolnet.org), IEARN (iearn.org), and ePals (epals.com/#/connections) suggest collaborations on content topics so students can share their interests and local information, and receive responses from children around the world. Kindnesses include things such as respecting others' viewpoints, and sharing homemade drawings and comments.

The My Hero Project (myhero.com) offers a collection of stories, short films, and art work, created by kids and adults around the world, which celebrate the best of humanity. Heroes come in all shapes and sizes, and they often emerge due to an unusual set of circumstances in which they find themselves acting, or reacting, compassionately. We all have the capacity to be heroes—a simple act of kindness to another can be a heroic act. When a child stands up to a bully on behalf of a classmate, that kindness *is* heroic. Sharing stories through film, text, and art broaden our knowledge of kind acts and contribute to an understanding that there are many wonderful people in the world who help build our shared perception of human kindness.

Activities

Here are several activities that foster kindness. Try them, and think about or write in your journal your thoughts and feelings about your experience. All of these activities can be adapted for use with children. Indeed, calling attention to being kind makes any place we work with children a more joyful space in which deeper learning can occur.

1. **R-E-S-P-E-C-T:** How many times have you told yourself that you are a loser, or that you made a stupid decision? Most people are their own harshest critics. Make a decision to treat yourself with respect. The next time you catch your inner critic coming out, stop and take a deep breath. Ask yourself how a friend would respond to you in this situation. What would she or he say or do? Odds are your friend would be far kinder than you are to yourself. So say or do the things you think your friend would say or do. You may also want to ask yourself what can be learned from the situation, and then move on.

2. **Laugh Out Loud:** You have heard the expression, "laughter is the best medicine," but did you know it is true? Laughter is powerful. It reduces stress, boosts your immune system, decreases levels of pain and fear, and more. Bottom line, it just makes you feel better. Be kind to yourself by giving yourself one (or more!) five-minute laughter breaks throughout the day. Watch funny video clips online, listen to a funny podcast, read jokes or other material intended to make you laugh. If you do not feel like laughing, do it anyway! As they say, "Fake it 'til you make it." The benefits in well-being are the same whether it is genuine laughter or initially pretend chuckles (Kataria, n.d.).

3. **There's Plenty of Kindness to Go Around:** People sometimes behave as though there is a finite amount of kindness in the world, so they save it for friends and family members. In reality, kindness is available in unlimited quantities, so spread it around! Everyone benefits from a little unexpected kindness. For the next

Activity ❶   R-E-S-P-E-C-T: Online Tools

Children often suffer from name-calling by others and themselves. You might discuss ideas for being kind, making lists of things with kids they can say to themselves and others that turn around that negative talk, as well as creating positive notes and cards for themselves and others as a special acknowledgment and demonstration of kindness.

- **The Little Memory** (thelittlememory.com/today): This online journal offers opportunities for recording thoughts, categorizing them, and sharing with others. The idea is that these are short notes rather than long entries. A thought for the day, something you are grateful for, or a positive note to yourself can be inspiring.

- **Lino** (en.linoit.com): Lino is a free sticky and photo sharing service that lets the user post sticky notes on a canvas using phones, web browsers, and tablets. Users can lay out pictures, notes, reminders, even videos—privately, or for others to see and contribute to as well. Crafting messages of inspiration and respect can help us set our tone for a good day.

- **Just Wink** (justwink.com): Just Wink offers a wide variety of cards that you can customize and send through email or Twitter, or you can pay for the site to print and send your card through "snail mail." There are cards for every occasion, including "just because" and blank ones, and all can be personalized with a message (several interesting fonts are available), photos, and a signature. You must sign up for an account, but there is no downloading required, and the online cards are free. Send yourself a card as a pat on the back for being you!

Activity ❷   LAUGH OUT LOUD: Online Tools

Building laughter into any setting where you work with children adds to a positive environment. Joke days, amusing videos, and funny stories let us relax and laugh, which encourages deep breathing—always a good thing.

- **Laughter Yoga** (laughteryoga.org): Founded by Dr. Madan Kataria, Laughter Yoga promotes laughing as a health benefit. At the website, download the free Laughter Yoga Guide, and check out several of the "Top 10 Laughter Exercises" as a start.

- **Puns for Kids** (examples.yourdictionary.com/examples-of-puns-for-kids.html): How do turtles talk with one another? By using their shell phones, of course! Word play through puns can help youngsters explore the English language while providing opportunities for laughter.

week, try this experiment: Enhance your interactions with your acquaintances by taking a moment to engage them in a brief conversation, by asking their opinion about something, or by making a point to look them in the eye when talking. You do not need to make them your new best friends, but even acquaintances appreciate being treated with kindness.

4. **Consistent Kindness:** Think about the people with whom you spend most of your time every day. You may be surprised to find that you interact with acquaintances more regularly than with friends and family. Many of your acquaintances may be people who provide some type of service such as a waitperson, hairdresser, barista, and so on. In the case of people who depend on tips to make a living wage, commit to regularly leaving a generous tip, say 20%. It is not much, but can make a big difference to the recipient. What about people you do not tip? What simple kindnesses can you show them regularly? Brainstorm a list and give your ideas a try. You will be the real beneficiary of this kindness.

5. **A Secret Kindness:** Want to boost your enjoyment of your day? Find a little thing you can do for a stranger who probably will not even know who did it. For example, you might pay the bridge toll for the car behind you. You could leave pennies in the cup at a cash register for the next person who needs one, pick up a bit of trash someone left behind, or return an orphan shopping cart to its place. There are many opportunities for small acts that truly make a difference in our collective lives. Keep a record of the good deeds you do, and see how it makes you feel.

6. **A Little Kindness:** Have you ever received too much change for a purchase and called attention to it? Was the person who gave you your change grateful? It is an act of kindness to right this kind of mistake—for the benefit of the cashier who would not balance their cash drawer at the end of the day, as well as for your own well-being. Doing the right thing is often such a small act, but the benefits can be huge. This might fall into the category of, "How would I feel if no one told me when I made a mistake such as this?" or simply seen as an act of goodwill. Think about the benefits, and bask in the warmth of your generosity.

7. **Reach Out and Touch Someone:** It is obvious when a friend or family member is experiencing a challenge, from a health issue to the loss of a dear friend, that a comforting phone call, email, or visit can make a difference. Just knowing someone cares is very valuable. But making a call or sending a note to say, "I'm thinking about you and wishing you well," can have a huge positive effect at *any* time—on the recipient as well as on your own psyche. It feels good to be noticed, acknowledged, and loved. Even without expecting or getting a response, you are better for having reached out.

8. **Tell Me a Story:** Birthdays, holidays, and other traditional celebrations often call for family gatherings. Taking the time to attend these events, even though it may be inconvenient or involve some expense, can make a huge difference in strengthening the relationships of everyone concerned. Maybe there is a difficult relative, or someone whose stories have been heard repeatedly. Showing interest and patience is a great kindness to someone who is lonely, generally isolated, or simply feels ignored or unimportant. We all have unique stories of our lives, and soliciting the telling of those stories might provide some insight into our own challenges. Listening can be a great gift, and the good feeling generated by truly paying attention to another person—family or friend—reaps huge benefits through our own feelings as well.

Questions for Reflection

1. In what ways are you already kind to others?

2. What is one thing you can do to show kindness to a stranger?

3. What difference does it make in your life to be kind?

4. Who in your family or network of friends could benefit today from an act of kindness?

5. What can you do to be kind to yourself?

Additional Resources

"Can Kindness Be Taught?" *The New York Times*, Richard Schiffman, December 14, 2017. nytimes.com/2017/12/14/well/family/kindness-curriculum-preschool.html

"Five Ways to Kindle Kindness from the Inside Out," Tara Cousineau, June 16, 2017. newharbinger.com/blog five-ways-kindle-kindness-inside-out

"Forget Survival of the Fittest: It Is Kindness That Counts," *Scientific American*, Dacher Keltner interviewed by David DiSalvo. scientificamerican.com/article/kindness-emotions-psychology

"Have You Listened to Your Self-Talk Lately?" *Psychology Today*, Toni Bernhard, April 5, 2011. tinyurl.com/yb7ouux5

"The Importance of Kindness," *Psychology Today*, Karyn Hall, December 4, 2017. psychologytoday.com/us/blog/pieces-mind/201712/the-importance-kindness

"Is Kindness Really Its Own Reward?" *Greater Good Magazine*, Emiliana R. Simon-Thomas, June 1, 2008. greatergood.berkeley.edu/article/item/is_kindness_really_its_own_reward

"One-Hundred-and-Three Random Acts of Kindness: Ideas to Inspire Kindness," Brad Aronson. bradaronson.com/acts-of-kindness

"Three Ways to Talk Yourself Up," *Reach Out Australia*. au.reachout.com/articles/how-to-practise-positive-self-talk

"Top 10 Scientific Benefits of Compassion," Emma M. Seppälä, December 15, 2013. tinyurl.com/y9tktosx

"Twenty Life Lessons from Mister Rogers," *Deseret News*, Sarah Petersen and Abby Stevens, October 14, 2013. tinyurl.com/ycfj74vj

ISTE Standards Connection

ISTE Standards for Educators 3a: Create experiences for learners to make positive, socially responsible contributions and exhibit empathetic behavior online that build relationships and community.

ISTE Standards for Education Leaders 1d: Model digital citizenship by critically evaluating online resources, engaging in civil discourse online and using digital tools to contribute to positive social change.

ISTE Standards for Education Leaders 3d: Support educators in using technology to advance learning that meets the diverse learning, cultural, and social-emotional needs of individual students.

ISTE Standards for Education Leaders 5c: Use technology to regularly engage in reflective practices that support personal and professional growth.

Creating an environment in which kindness is valued—online and offline—provides a more positive learning environment when working with children in a variety of settings. Acts of kindness increase well-being and help build understanding of others locally and globally.

6

Movement

🐚 In his book *A More Beautiful Question*, author Warren Berger describes the plight of Van Phillips, who enjoyed an active, athletic lifestyle until he lost his left foot in a water-skiing accident. Phillips refused to be satisfied with the prosthetics he tried because they did not allow him to return to what he loved best—running and other active sports. He asked questions, explored possible solutions, and eventually came up with a design that is now known around the world. Sometimes called the *cheetah foot*, his prosthetic devices allow users to run, climb, and participate in other athletic activities, including the Olympic games (2016).

Overview

Moving shows that we are alive! Our bodies benefit greatly from movement throughout the day. According to Paula Youmell, a registered nurse with a background in holistic health (n.d.), "Not only does regular activity strengthen your muscles and improve heart and lung function, but it can also reduce your risk of major diseases, stimulate the growth of new brain cells, and even add years to your life."

The benefits of moving—even small movements—are myriad. According to Dr. Srini Pillay (2016), "Changing your posture, breathing, and rhythm can all change your brain, thereby reducing stress, depression, and anxiety, and leading to a feeling of well-being." He goes on to say, "Your mind and body are intimately connected. And while your brain *is* the master control system for your body's movement, the way you *move* can also affect the way you think and feel."

In our sedentary society, even small movements become important. Simply getting up from sitting for any length of time and moving around helps. Of course, being able to go outside is even better! We come back to our work with more energy and a renewed sense of purpose because our bodies feel better.

Let's take a deeper look at the impact of exercise on the body, the mind, and relationships.

Body

It seems obvious that exercise—or lack thereof—has a profound effect on our bodies. Some people spend many hours building the bodies they want; bodies that look strong and toned; bodies that can lift heavy weights, run many miles, or win pugilistic contests. However, most of us do not have the desire or ability to spend time in this way. We want to be healthy, prevent diseases and the effects of aging, and feel in control of how we look, feel, and move.

Harvard Health Publishing offers daily health tips, such as, "Motivate yourself to exercise. It can be tough to be active. Try doing something fun that involves activity, such as volunteering at an animal shelter or delivering meals to people who can't leave their homes. It doesn't have to be much; just 20 minutes a day makes a huge difference" (Harvard Health Publishing: Harvard Medical School, 2015).

Far too many schools have cut physical education classes in favor of remediation and work on improving test scores. Laura Moser (2016) offers an optimistic perspective: "With the passage of the new Every Student Succeeds Act, there is some hope that schools will develop a more coherent commitment to physical fitness. PE programs are now eligible for Title I funding." Happily, some schools across the country are making sure students have meaningful physical education experiences that include understanding how our bodies work, the benefits of working together, as well as an awareness of how physical activities can improve learning and other aspects of life. In the video, *The New PE Runs on Fitness, Not Competition* (Edutopia, 2008), the George Lucas Educational Foundation shares stories from a number of schools in which a variety of new physical activities are included in PE classes. The video emphasizes why physical fitness is important and how other skills can be obtained by working together and thinking critically about physical challenges.

Mind

Alvaro Fernandez (2007) reminds us that "things that exercise your body can also help sharpen your brain: physical exercise

WHERE TO FIND RESEARCH ON MOVEMENT

We move every day, but that does not necessarily mean we are comfortable with more formal exercise activities, or that we understand why movement is so important. These websites offer all kinds of information related to exercise and the benefits of even limited activity.

- **Harvard Health Publishing:** Harvard Medical School: Exercise and Fitness (health.harvard.edu/topics/exercise-and-fitness): This site offers links to many articles on movement, as well as other topics such as men's health, women's health, heart health, mind and mood, staying healthy, pain, cancer, diseases, and conditions.

- **Mayo Clinic:** Healthy Lifestyle: Fitness (tinyurl.com/ych2a7bg): The Mayo Clinic site provides links to related articles and videos on fitness, as well as links to their Healthy Living Program and the Mayo Clinic Health Letter.

- **University of California, Berkeley Wellness** (berkeleywellness.com): The site includes articles on a variety of topics with the themes of fitness, supplements, healthy eating, healthy minds, healthy communities, and self-care. You can subscribe to a free online newsletter as well.

enhances neurogenesis, at any age!" In addition to movement, his ten habits of highly effective brains include laughing, friendships, positive thoughts, travel, and learning something new on a continuous basis.

The Literacy and Language Center (2016) suggests that movement breaks during class affect efficiency in learning, stress relief, mood elevation, social perks, class cohesion; they also address the role of oxygen in learning.

Thinking about what types of movement keep kids engaged is also important. Dr. Gregory D. Myer, Director of Desearch and The Human Performance Laboratory for the Division of Sports Medicine at Cincinnati Children's Hospital Medical Center, asserts that "[the] focus on exercise quantity in youth may limit considerations of qualitative aspects of programme design which include (1) skill development, (2) socialisation and (3) enjoyment of exercise." (2015, January). He says kids between five and seven begin to compare their skills to their peers, and they start avoiding physical activity if they feel they do not measure up. "First, it's gotta be fun or they're not gonna do it. Then we have to create some skill-based movements in it and teach them how to do it. It has to be fun and in short bursts. And often they are missing the strength-building exercises. Strength and motor-skills building go hand-in-hand and are often ignored in these guidelines for kids" (Myer, as cited in Westervelt, 2015).

Amy Cuddy's research brings together mind and body. She is a social psychologist, interested in body language—what we communicate to each other by facial expression or stance. She and her colleagues found that assuming what they call a "power pose," such as Wonder Woman's iconic hands-on-hips stance, or standing or running with hands thrown up in the air in a V-shaped posture of triumph, can change body hormones. Standing (or sitting) for two minutes in a power pose increases testosterone—the dominance hormone—and decreases cortisol—the stress hormone. Cuddy suggests taking a power pose for two minutes in the bathroom, behind your office door, or some other private place before heading into a stressful situation such as leading a class, giving a presentation, or attending a job interview. She suggests we fake it 'til we make it, or, better yet, fake it until we become it. "Our bodies can change our minds," she says (2012).

Relationships

Researchers Joanne Lumsden, Lynden K. Miles, and C. Neil Macrae (2014) launched a study to evaluate participants in synchronous and asynchronous movements with another and how it affected their self-esteem. They report that "the results revealed that individuals felt better about themselves following a period of synchronous compared to asynchronous movement, while they also perceived a greater self-other overlap with their partner" (p. 1). Walking with a friend, for instance, may have greater health benefits than walking alone—which is also something good to do!

Team sports can promote good relationships. When we commit to playing on a team, we understand that others rely on us to show up and participate. Good team players see the abilities of the team as more important than a single player's strengths. Winning teams have figured out how to work together so each member's strengths contribute to the whole, and each member's weaknesses can be addressed and move toward becoming strengths.

The attitudes and participation of parents and other adults in children's lives make huge differences with kids. While Dr. Myer (Westervelt, 2015) offers advice to parents, it can apply to anyone: "Work on some of these motor skills that are a little more advanced: Kicking, throwing, or shooting a basketball. So that [your] child gets more opportunities when they're not in front of their peers. You show them how it can be fun and create games around it. That's when the child will say, 'Hey, this is not so bad,' and they'll start to work on those skills independently. Then they'll go back into the class and it gives them an opportunity to catch up. And I think the parents need to be out there moving as much as the kids. That's probably a different story, but the benefits to the family will be even greater by focusing on the activities of their children."

All of this probably makes sense, but how can it really work? There are challenges. Hopefully, you will find strategies in the following sections to address your concerns.

The Real-World Connection

There are plenty of opinions from a plethora of sources that insist on the right number of minutes or hours, and the kind of exercise, we all should get every day or week for our health. Some say 30 minutes a day, three times a week. Some say five days a week, including rest days. Some say 10 minutes a day with a special machine or particular short set of exercises will do it. Other questions abound. What time of day is the best? What are the best shoes to wear? Does yoga count if I do not break a sweat? Are team sports better because of the built-in accountability factor? Each individual will answer all these questions for him- or herself. Perhaps the best idea is to try out a lot of physical activities, see which ones you like and will stick with, and build a healthy habit around them. Or consider the activities you enjoyed as a child, and see if those still speak to you or could be adapted to your time and health today.

Of course, before you start on a new exercise regimen, you will want to consider checking with your doctor or other health care provider to make sure there are no physical or other considerations that might preclude your participation. When you get the green light, go for it. Find out what you love doing and do it! Two things to think about are forming new habits and time.

Habits

James Clear (2018) asserts that it's a myth to suggest that a new habit becomes permanent in 21 days. Indeed, "how long it takes a new habit to form can vary widely depending on the behavior, the person, and the circumstances." He goes on to say that "habits are a process and not an event." By understanding that it will take time to change, committing to doing the work, and doing the best you can to improve regularly, you will get there, and your new habit will stick. There is no need to be hard on yourself when you inevitably slip up—keep going, start again, and you'll find success. Clear says, "Embrace the long, slow walk to greatness and focus on putting in your reps."

The "habit loop" has been defined by MIT researchers as being made up of three components: the cue, the routine or behavior itself, and the reward. Charles Duhigg (2013) suggests that the way to break a bad habit is to thoughtfully identify each aspect of the habit loop, and then specify the action you will take to alter it. When he explored his own habit of going to get a chocolate chip cookie every day between 3:00 and 3:30 p.m., he came to realize that the reward was not the cookie but getting to talk with colleagues for a bit when he got the cookie in the cafeteria. By understanding the true reward, he was able to get up from his desk and find colleagues to chat with without having to go to the cafeteria.

Duhigg proposes going through the process of identifying the routine, experimenting with different rewards, and isolating the cue. This last is perhaps most important, because it is often difficult to pick out the trigger for our activity. Making note of circumstances such as where you are, who you are with, what time it is, and your emotional state can provide clues. After all this, he says, make a plan ahead of time to plan for the cue, decide on the behavior, and identify the reward that will work.

Gabriele Oettingen's (2014) work on motivation provides a specific technique for handling change effectively and achieving results: WOOP—the four-step practice that her research has shown really works. The W stands for *Wish:* What is your fondest wish? Think about it for a few minutes until it is clear in your mind. Then look at the *Outcomes* you would like to achieve if this wish came true. However, you will most likely encounter *Obstacles* as you work toward getting your wish, so consider them. Then, create your *Plan* for overcoming the obstacles. Oettingen's research has shown that thinking positively about changes we want to make is unrealistic if that is all we do, but when we confront the obstacles that might arise and make a plan with if/then statements, we have a much better chance at success. There are many videos online, as well as the WOOP website (woopmylife.org) that provide information, specific instructions for each step, and more.

Time

But there are not enough minutes in the day to do what I'm doing already. How can I make time to add exercise? James Clear advises very small steps. Timothy Pychyl (2008) posits, "It is not as effective to make yourself a 'to do' list of goal intentions as it is to decide *how, when,* and *where* you are going to accomplish each of the tasks you need to get done. In fact, a recently published study reveals that stating an *implementation intention* (a term coined by New York University professor of psychology Peter Gollwitzer) of when and where you'll act will make it more likely that you'll keep your appointments."

Technology and Movement

Technology offers a variety of tools to help keep track of physical activity, heart rate, sleep, weight, and more. What's wrong with that? Nothing—unless you become fixated on the device and find yourself engaged in unhealthy activities. For example, do you find yourself avoiding some forms of exercise you love because they won't count as steps? Or checking your device more often than you check for messages on your phone? Samantha Cooper (2016) first loved her smartwatch, but later found that it fostered competition and obsession. When she gave it up, she returned to enjoying the variety of exercise programs she had earlier engaged in, as well as the aspects of them that allowed her to destress. Her advice: you may not be ready to throw away your device, but at least consider whether it has become a compulsion, and if so, if it is worth it.

While the online world allows us to be in touch with others for many reasons, including sharing health goals, challenges and successes, it never really takes the place of meeting people face-to-face, walking and talking together, playing on a live team, or sharing time in a wellness class. Certainly, learn all you can, sort through the sometimes controversial research, and come to your own conclusions about your health and exercise.

There is a lot of information available online regarding exercise programs, tools, and devices. Videos, podcasts, and online courses provide many ways to learn exercises, explore different movement practices, and refine technique.

Research by Jane Collingwood (2018), Mike Bundrant (2015), and others on the power of music to reduce stress and facilitate meditation and sleep has been confirmed. Soft music can facilitate feeling less depression, reduce the experience of pain, and promote healing. Indeed, Lauren Gelman and Michelle Crouch (n.d.) explain that "listening to music promotes the body's production of an antibody (called immunoglobulin A) that attacks viruses and bacteria, as well as natural 'killer cells,' which kill invading viruses and cancerous cells." Listening to music also produces dopamine, which has a calming effect. Music can also provide encouraging backdrops for exercise programs. Download your favorite song, plug in those ear buds, and get moving!

Our recommendations: move in ways that fit your goals, work at your own rate, experiment with different programs, and do what's fun and interesting. We agree it is not easy to make changes, create new habits, and exercise consistently. Ultimately, we like what Mark Sisson has to say about it: "The single best exercise there is, hands down, is the one you'll do" (2014).

Activities

The following activities include suggestions for moving as individuals or with partners or groups; having a variety of ways to move will keep your practice interesting and enjoyable. They can be adapted for youngsters, as well as expanded in some instances into group activities.

1. **May I Have This Dance?** Whether you prefer dancing with a partner, in a group, or by yourself, there are many choices available for moving to music. Ballroom, line, square, country western, Latin— all styles offer plenty of physical action as well as brain workouts. Many short videos of dance style instruction can be found on YouTube for an introduction to the steps and for practice at home before you venture out to venues for dance in your area.

2. **Be a Team Player:** Another way to participate in group exercise is to join a team sport such as softball, hockey, volleyball, or basketball. Along with the health benefits, being a member of a team develops players' resiliency, responsibility, social and leadership skills, and ability to think quickly and make effective decisions. The important thing with team sports is to remember that it is just a game, and this is an opportunity to have fun.

3. **It's the Little Things That Count:** Opportunities abound for small, concentrated movements every day. Sitting, standing in line, cooking, driving, or doing the myriad activities that consume our waking hours can become times to make a move. Move your toes and feet, focus on hand and wrist movements, walk with the back of your neck straight. If you spend a lot of time sitting, stand up every hour or so and move around. When you are waiting in line, stand with your feet hip width apart and outer edges parallel to feel proper alignment.

4. **Home Work:** If you are tired of working out at the gym or trying to figure out when you can fit in the time, consider creating your own space and time at home. Plan your own workout—and vary it as you see fit—with the aid of online suggestions as well as your own experience. Many online classes, DVDs, and TV programs offer a wide range of targeted exercise plans, depending on your interest, focus, capacity, and health. Pluses of home workouts include that you can play your music as loud as you would like, minimal equipment is needed, and your house is always open. Keep a workout journal and notice how you feel over time.

5. **Let's Play!** What's your favorite partner or group activity? Badminton? Ping pong? Bowling? Tennis? Tether ball? Horseshoes? Croquet? Billiards? Fencing? Boxing? Darts? So many possibilities! A number of these activities can be played with more than two people, but all of them offer opportunities for two people to get into it together and have some fun, while increasing dexterity, stamina, and eye-hand coordination.

6. **Walk with a Buddy:** Going for a walk is the easiest exercise to implement—no special equipment needed, and you do not have to travel anywhere. Experts recommend walking 30 minutes, five days a week to stay fit, improve health, and lose weight. So why don't we? It is easy to intend to walk, then get distracted. Note this: People who walk with a partner are more motivated and accountable than people who walk alone. So find a friend to walk with, or walk with different partners during the week. The health benefits are well worth the effort. The point is to get out there and get walking.

7. **Hit the Gym:** Membership in a gym can offer a lot of choices with equipment specifically designed for particular exercises and physical benefits, as well as flexible scheduling for your workouts. Often supervision or a personal trainer can increase the effectiveness and safety of your gym experience. Machines, classes, weights, swimming pools—most gyms offer a variety of ways to exercise. You will also meet others engaged in the same purpose of improving physical abilities. If you go at the same time every day, you will probably recognize the regulars and perhaps make new friends—which can help keep the incentive high to return.

Activity ① MAY I HAVE THIS DANCE?: Online Tools

Activities that incorporate singing and dancing as "brain breaks," as well as ideas for bringing movement into curriculum areas, increase opportunities for children to move.

- **Brain Breaks Action Songs for Children** (bit.ly/2PJfxTN): Songs and dances for kids of all ages offer a break from sedentary work, and energizes them when they get back to work as well! The Learning Station (learningstationmusic.com) offers a YouTube channel with lots of songs, dances, and links to their CDs, and if you go directly to Brain Breaks Action Songs for Children, you can choose from a long list to get everyone up and moving!

- **21 Awesome Ways to Get Your Students Moving During Learning Center Time** (bit.ly/2I5gHsO): While the actual title refers to students, the activities can be used in any setting where there are children: Ball-Toss Spelling and Fitness Dice are only two of the ideas this website offers to get children moving and engaging in learning through movement.

- **iMovie** (apple.com/imovie), **Movie Maker** (bit.ly/2LzKHKf), or other programs, such as **VideoPad** (nchsoftware.com/videopad/index.html), let students make videos to share with their classmates to get them moving!

Activity ② BE A TEAM PLAYER: Online Tools

- **Active Kids: Five Tips to Be a Good Team Player** (bit.ly/2BUkpCW): See a slideshow with tips for team members to get the most out of their team play. The suggestions can be discussed with teams, so kids can share their ideas as well.

- **Kids Playing for Kids** (kidsplayingforkids.org): Teams of healthy kids "adopt" chronically ill kids so they can experience playing on a team. Benefits for the healthy kids include building empathy for others with health challenges and understanding that they can make a difference by including and helping others. .

- **Grown & Flown** (grownandflown.com/push-kids-to-play-team-sports): This website provides reasons for kids to play team sports. Aimed at adults, it offers points that parents can share with their children on the benefits of playing on a team.

8. **Group Classes for Individuals:** Attending classes for specific exercises might be appealing to you—alone or with a group of friends. Many organizations offer exercise classes that are open to the public. For example, check your local YMCA and YWCA, city or town parks and recreation programs, senior centers, and more.

Questions for Reflection

1. How many ways can you incorporate small movements into your day?

2. What new skill or activity will you begin to learn today?

3. How will you fit regular exercise into your life?

4. What are some movement activities you can do with a friend or friends?

5. What process for creating or changing a habit will you try?

Additional Resources

"Intermittent Movement Benefits Your Health. Here's How to Get More of It into Your Work Day," Joseph Mercola, April 11, 2014. tinyurl.com/y9lpkuv3

"Nutritious Movement," Katy Bowman, 2018. nutritiousmovement.com

"Thirteen Mental Health Benefits of Exercise," *HuffPost*, Sophia Breene, December 6, 2017. tinyurl.com/y8y7hhzf

ISTE Standards Connection

ISTE Standards for Educators 1a: Set professional learning goals to explore and apply pedagogical approaches made possible by technology and reflect on their effectiveness.

ISTE Standards for Education Leaders 2a: Engage education stakeholders in developing and adopting a shared vision for using technology to improve student success, informed by the learning sciences.

ISTE Standards for Education Leaders 5a: Set goals to remain current on emerging technologies for learning, innovations in pedagogy and advancements in the learning sciences.

There is no shortage of technology tools that address movement, help build healthy habits, and allow adults and students to share ideas for healthy living, with new examples emerging daily. Adults can provide safe forums for youngsters' explorations to increase their health and welfare.

7

Where to Go from Here

Life is not all "rainbows and unicorns"— never has been, never will be. The point of this book is not to pretend that there is some magical path to a euphoric state in which everything is perfect all the time. We chose to include the attitudes and strategies in this book because practicing them increases the likelihood that, when something bad happens (and it will), you will have the resilience to get through whatever transpires.

We Always Have Choices

Stoicism, a school of Hellenistic philosophy, was founded during the third century BCE and is still practiced today. A key tenet of Stoic philosophy is the ability to identify those life events or challenges that are within an individual's control and those which are not (Control and Choice, 2018). Why is this an important distinction? People spend an inordinate amount of time worrying about potential or actual events over which they have absolutely no control, increasing their levels of anxiety and stress for no verifiable gain. Oddly enough, they often fail to recognize those times where they *do* have a certain amount of control over a situation, and they abdicate their autonomy in the process.

Many of the difficult life challenges faced by human beings, such as the death of a loved one, an economic depression, or a natural disaster, are completely out of an individual's control. Any one of these events could result in devastating loss. Stoics believe that unimaginable hurts can also make a person stronger—the end result often depends on how an individual chooses to respond (Sharpe, 2017).

Just as people are always able to make choices about how they react in any given situation, we have agency when it comes to defining how the use of technology impacts our lives. We believe technology can be a positive force in people's lives, but we understand that this does not happen on its own. Pew Research Center and Elon University conducted a survey and the results of that survey support our belief: 47% of survey participants think the role digital technology plays in their lives over the next decade will help people's well-being; 32% think people's well-being will be harmed by digital technology; and 21% do not think there will be much change one way or the other. When asked to explain their answers, many respondents acknowledged both positive and negative aspects of technology use in daily life, but they also suggested remedies that can be employed to counter the negatives. Here are some of the themes in their responses.

- **Positive:** Various technologies make it possible for people to easily communicate with one another, to readily access information, and more, on demand. Online commerce has revolutionized many businesses and made goods more accessible to consumers. Ready access to up-to-date health and scientific information is beneficial to many people.

- **Negative:** Overuse of technology may result in declines in critical thinking skills as well as increased stress or depression. There is concern about digital addiction. Some users become obsessed with digital technology at the expense of their real lives. Dangers related to loss of personal privacy were also mentioned.

- **Possible Solutions:** Be thoughtful about how people will use and be impacted by new technologies as those technologies are being developed. Provide formal instructional in thoughtful use of technology. Recognize that people need to learn how to incorporate new technologies into their lives and give them time to work through these changes (Anderson & Rainie, 2018).

If we want technology to enhance people's lives, we need to be willing to take an ongoing, honest look at how it is used, and how that use can be leveraged to add value to the lives of users.

The American public was made aware of a prime example of technology misuse when the Facebook/Cambridge Analytica scandal broke in March 2018. Cambridge Analytica, a London-based voter-profiling company, contracted with Robert Mercer to profile personalities of American voters and use those profiles to influence their voting decisions. Although Cambridge Analytica had developed the tools to do this, the company did not have the data it needed to create the profiles. As a result, the company bought data that had been collected from 50 million Facebook profiles by an outside researcher, who had claimed he was using the data for research purposes. At no time did any of the parties involved get explicit permission from Facebook users to mine and use their information (Rosenberg et al., 2018).

This is just the tip of the data-mining misuse iceberg. Does this mean that we need to avoid social media and other online services? Not at all. But it does mean that we need to pay particular attention to the possible remedies identified in the Pew Research Center/Elon University survey mentioned previously. For instance, current practice for app developers is to use brain research to design apps that capitalize on users' fear of missing out on something new (FOMO). The default setting for notifications is set to "on." Scrolling through news feeds frequently results in a spinning wheel graphic that implies new content is being downloaded. Information is presented in a story format that is even more appealing to readers than regular posts. Users can succumb to these built-in lures, or they can learn to manage apps and make conscious decisions to avoid falling into the app "black hole."

How can a person learn to make better decisions about technology use? Adults may be on their own, although it would not hurt to ask their employers' human resources departments to offer workshops or other training on this topic. Use the rationale that happier employees are more productive employees, and that informed use of technology reduces stress, anxiety, depression, insomnia, and other negative side effects of staring at screens all day. The technology sections in chapters 1 through 6 of this book are also a source of good information for readers who want to refine their personal use of technology.

Readers who work with children will want to explore resources designed to help youngsters develop good habits when it comes to technology. Consider incorporating these resources into the curriculum used to teach digital citizenship skills. The features that keep adults coming back to their smartphones are the same features that appeal to kids. Take another look at the information provided in the technology sections in chapters 1 through 6 and think about how it relates to the children or teens in your life. The important thing to remember is that they will not figure this out on their own—it is up to adults to instruct and model healthy technology habits.

Practicing What We Preach

Just as there is no way to live a life without challenges, there is no one approach to cultivating changes in attitude that will work for everyone. We thought it would be helpful to share how we each address the six areas of well-being covered in this book.

Exercise has been a regular part of Susan's routine for many years. In the early 1990s, she started practicing an occasional anonymous act of kindness. It was not such a big deal; whenever she purchased a cup of coffee for herself, she would leave extra money for the barista or counter person to provide a complimentary coffee to a customer who looked like she or he could use a boost. She stepped up her game with acts of kindness when she read about 29 Gifts, a project that encourages participants to give a gift each day for 29 days (Walker, 2009). These gifts were sometimes tangible, sometimes acts of kindness.

This was Susan's first exposure to the idea of daily practice of behaviors that could impact her life as well as others.

In working to learn more about what attitudes and behaviors contribute to a sense of well-being, Susan was reminded of the power of gratitude, being positive, getting focused, and empathy. One idea kept popping up in her reading—the importance of daily practice—so she decided to start doing at least one thing every day in each of the six areas. To hold herself accountable, Susan keeps a daily journal. Each evening before bedtime, she takes a few minutes to list each area and write how she addressed it that particular day. She lists three things for which she is grateful, one positive thing that happened, what she did to get focused, how she exercised, an act of kindness she made, and a way she demonstrated empathy. It takes approximately ten minutes and has been very helpful in shaping Susan's overall sense of well-being.

Sara has approached things in a way that suits her lifestyle. There are areas she acts on daily and others she addresses less frequently, but still regularly. Unlike Susan, she does not keep a journal, but she holds herself accountable by being conscious of her behavior throughout the day. Examples of Sara's daily practice include keeping her own gratitude jar (see chapter 1, activity 3), making a daily checklist to keep focused, and striving to treat herself and others with kindness and empathy every day. She attends exercise classes twice weekly and regularly spends time with friends who enrich her life. Sara keeps her focus on being positive by subscribing to (and reading) several e-newsletters that send positive messages and articles her way daily.

As you can see, although we are focusing on the same six areas, we each have our own way of incorporating a practice of well-being into our lives. You can do the same.

Making a Plan

As mentioned in the previous section, there are projects and programs that recommend trying a new behavior for varying periods of time. Susan started with 29 days, but other suggested time frames run between 21 and 30 days. One study from University College London suggests that people take anywhere from 18 to 254 days to form a new habit, with the average being 76 days (Lally et al., 2010). Rather than deciding to try something for a set number of days, we recommend the following steps:

1. Decide which strategy or strategies you want to practice regularly.

2. Commit to a schedule for implementation (e.g., daily, weekly, something else).

3. Identify what you will do to hold yourself accountable (e.g., journal, diary, tell someone else).

4. Get started.

5. Adjust your plan as needed.

The most important thing is to commit and act. If the plan is too ambitious, it can be pared back. If the plan is too limited, it can be expanded. Keep this book in a place where it can be located easily to use as a reference for new activity ideas or to remember why certain strategies are helpful. Your personal plan is not carved in stone, so feel free to change things as needed.

While our target audience is adults who work with children in a variety of different settings, many of these activities are appropriate for use with youngsters. As you become comfortable with the material presented in this book, we encourage you to incorporate these practices into your work. We also have created a LiveBinder of Well-Being Resources (livebinders.com/play/play?id=1530092) that readers are welcome to use and share. We do update resources periodically, so keep coming back!

Additional Resources

"The Scientists Who Make Apps Addictive," *The Economist 1843*, Ian Leslie, October/November, 2016. 1843magazine.com/features/the-scientists-who-make-apps-addictive

"To Serve a Free Society, Social Media Must Evolve Beyond Data Mining," *The Conversation*, Aram Sinnreich & Barbara Romzeck, April 11, 2018. tinyurl.com/yd7pvfb5

"What Is 'Brain-Hacking'? Tech Insiders on Why You Should Care,"
    60 Minutes, Anderson Cooper, April 9, 2017. cbsnews.com/news/
    brain-hacking-tech-insiders-60-minutes

References

American Psychiatric Association. (2017, August 4). Practicing gratitude can be good for mental health and well-being [Blog]. Retrieved from https://www.psychiatry.org/news-room/apa-blogs/apa-blog/2017/08/practicing-gratitude-can-be-good-for-mental-health-and-well-being

American Red Cross. (2018). Contact loved ones. Retrieved from https://www.redcross.org/get-help/disaster-relief-and-recovery-services/contact-and-locate-loved-ones.html

Anderson, J, & Rainie, L. (2018, April 17). The future of well-being in a tech-saturated world. Pew Research Center. Retrieved from http://www.pewinternet.org/2018/04/17/the-future-of-well-being-in-a-tech-saturated-world/

Asano, E. (2017, January 4). How much time do people spend on social media? [Infographic]. *Social Media Today*. Retrieved from https://www.socialmediatoday.com/marketing/how-much-time-do-people-spend-social-media-infographic

Barr, S. (2018, October 11). Six ways social media negatively affects your mental health. Retrieved from https://www.independent.co.uk/life-style/health-and-families/social-media-mental-health-negative-effects-depression-anxiety-addiction-memory-a8307196.html

Batson, C. (2009). These things called empathy: Eight related but distinct phenomena. In J. Decety & W. Ickes (Eds.), *The social neuroscience of empathy* (3–16). Cambridge, MA: MIT Press.

Berger, W. (2016). *A more beautiful question: The power of inquiry to spark breakthrough ideas*. New York, NY: Bloomsbury.

Beyer, J. (2017, June 28). How would you answer this question? [blog]. Retrieved from tinyurl.com/y8zs4kdg

Borowsky, H. (2015, October 9). Toolkit for promoting empathy. *Start Empathy*. Retrieved from startempathy.org/resources/toolkit

Brownstein, R. (2015, October 10). America's growing pessimism. *The Atlantic*. Retrieved from https://www.theatlantic.com/politics/archive/2015/10/americans-pessimism-future/409564/

Bryson, M. (2018, February 27). Won't you be my neighbor? The leadership secrets of Mr. Rogers. Retrieved from gordontraining.com/leadership/wont-neighbor-leadership-secrets-mister-rogers

Bundrant, M. (2015, April). Four scientific studies that show music decreasing stress and promoting healing. *PsychCentral*. Retrieved from tinyurl.com/yboh4667

Burton, N. (2012, May 24). Man's search for meaning: Meaning as a cure for depression and other ills. *Psychology Today*. Retrieved from https://www.psychologytoday.com/us/blog/hide-and-seek/201205/mans-search-meaning

Clear, J. (2018). How long does it actually take to form a new habit? (Backed by science). Retrieved from jamesclear.com/new-habit

Collingwood, J. (2018, March 22). The power of music to reduce stress. *PsychCentral*. Retrieved from psychcentral.com/lib/the-power-of-music-to-reduce-stress

Control and Choice. (2018). Retrieved from https://dailystoic.com/control-and-choice

Cooper, S. (2016, March 31). How my Fitbit turned into an unhealthy obsession. Retrieved from spoonuniversity.com/lifestyle/how-my-fitbit-turned-into-an-unhealthy-obsession

Cottle, T. J. (1993, Spring). The art of distraction. *The Antioch Review, 51*(2), 284–293. Retrieved from https://www.jstor.org/stable/4612732?seq=1#page_scan_tab_contents

Cuddy, A. (2012, June). *Amy Cuddy: Your body language may shape who you are* [Video file]. Retrieved from ted.com/talks/amy_cuddy_your_body_language_shapes_who_you_are

Detrick, R. (2017, November). All the feelings: Seeking to understand empathy, *California English*, (23)1, 6–7. San Diego, CA: California Association of Teachers of English (CATE).

Doyle, B. (2014, January 19). 365 days of thank you: Brian Doyle at TEDxYouth@San Diego 2013 [Video file]. Retrieved from youtube. com/watch?time_continue=501&v=QNfAnkojhoE

Duhigg, C. (2013, August 18). The power of habit: Charles Duhigg at TEDx Teachers College [Video file]. Retrieved from youtube.com/ watch?v=OMbsGBlpP30

Duhigg, C. (2018). How habits work. Retrieved from charlesduhigg. com/how-habits-work

Dunion, P. (2016, November 11). The art of self-forgiveness [Blog]. Retrieved from https://www.huffingtonpost.com/paul-dunion-edd-lpc/the-art-of-self-forgiveness_b_8537240.html

Edutopia. (2008, May 28). The new PE runs on fitness not competition [Video file]. Retrieved from edutopia.org/video/ new-pe-runs-fitness-not-competition

Ekman, P. (2010, June 21). Paul Ekman's taxonomy of compassion. *Greater Good Magazine*. Retrieved from greatergood.berkeley.edu/ article/item/paul_ekmans_taxonomy_of_compassion

Emmons, R. (2007, June 1). Pay it forward. *Greater Good Magazine*. Retrieved from greatergood.berkeley.edu/article/item/ pay_it_forward

Emmons, R. (2008, November). *Thanks! How practicing gratitude can make you happier*. New York, NY: Houghton Mifflin.

Emmons, R. (2010, November 16). Why gratitude is good. *Greater Good Magazine*. Retrieved from greatergood.berkeley.edu/article/item/ why_gratitude_is_good

Emmons, R. (2013, September 12). How gratitude can help you through hard times. *Daily Good*. Retrieved from http: //www.dailygood.org/story/532/how-gratitude-can-help-you-through-hard-times-robert-emmons

"Empathy Quiz." (2018). Retrieved from greatergood.berkeley.edu/ quizzes/take_quiz/empathy

Fernandez, A. (2007, August 22). The ten habits of highly effective brains [Blog]. *SharpBrains*. Retrieved from sharpbrains.com/ blog/2007/08/22/10-habits-of-highly-effective-brains

Field, P. (2015, April 20). Five researched-based reasons to be kind. *HuffPost*. Retrieved from https://www.huffpost.com/entry/ kindness-research_b_7054652

Flaxington, B. D. (2015, August 28). Distracted living: Take your attention back! *Psychology Today*. Retrieved from https://www.psychologytoday.com/us/blog/understand-other-people/201508/distracted-living

Frank, C. (n.d.). Why does daydreaming get such a bad rap? Retrieved from webmd.com/balance/features/why-does-daydreaming-get-such-bad-rap#1

Frankl, V.E. (1985, originally published in 1946). *Man's search for meaning*. New York, NY. Washington Square Press.

Fredrickson, B. L. (2004, August 17). The broaden-and-build theory of positive emotions. Retrieved from ncbi.nlm.nih.gov/pmc/articles/PMC1693418/pdf/15347528.pdf

Fredrickson, B. L. (2011, June 20). *Positive emotions open our mind* [Video file]. Retrieved from youtube.com/watch?time_continue=497&v=Z7dFDHzV36g

Fredrickson, B. L., Tugade, M. M., Waugh, C. E., & Larkin, G. R. (2003, February). What good are positive emotions in crises? A prospective study of resilience and emotions following the terrorist attacks on the United States on September 11, 2001. *Journal of Personality and Social Psychology, (84)*2, 365–76. Retrieved from ncbi.nlm.nih.gov/pmc/articles/PMC2755263

Gazzaley, A. & Rosen, L. D. (2016). *The distracted mind: Ancient brains in a high-tech world*. Cambridge, MA: MIT Press.

Gelman, L. & Crouch, M. (n.d.) Twenty-one hidden health benefits music lovers wish you knew. Retrieved from besthealthmag.ca/best-you/wellness/health-benefits-music/view-all

Gold, T. (2002). *Open your mind, open your life: A book of eastern wisdom*. Kansas City, MO: Lionstead Press, Inc.

Goleman, D. (2010). Hot to help. In D. Keltner, J. March, & J. A. Smith (Eds.), *The compassionate instinct: The science of human goodness* (171–76). New York, NY: W. W. Norton & Company.

Gordon, M. (2011, July 27). The wisdom of babies. *Greater Good Magazine*. Retrieved from greatergood.berkeley.edu/article/item/wisdom_of_babies

Hamilton, D. R (2017, February 14). The five side effects of kindness. Retrieved from https://drdavidhamilton.com/the-5-side-effects-of-kindness-2/

Harvard Health Publishing: Harvard Medical School. (2015, June). Motivate yourself to exercise. Retrived from https://www.health.harvard.edu/daily_health_tip/motivate-yourself-to-exercise

Helliwell, J., Layard, R., & Sachs, J. (2017, March). *World happiness report 2017*. New York, NY: Sustainable Development Solutions Network. Retrieved from worldhappiness.report/ed/2017

Horton, A. (2018, March 14). Perhaps tired of winning, the United States falls in World Happiness rankings–again. Retrieved from https://www.washingtonpost.com/news/worldviews/wp/2018/03/14/perhaps-tired-of-winning-the-united-states-falls-in-world-happiness-rankings-again/?utm_term=.8eb458a9f762

Jantz, G. L. (2016, May 16). The power of positive self-talk [Blog]. *Psychology Today*. Retrieved from psychologytoday.com/us/blog/hope-relationships/201605/the-power-positive-self-talk

John, Y. J. (2016, March 21). The "Streetlight Effect": A Metaphor for Knowledge and Ignorance. *3 Quarks Daily*. Retrieved from https://www.3quarksdaily.com/3quarksdaily/2016/03/the-streetlight-effect-a-metaphor-for-knowledge-and-ignorance.html

Kataria, Madan (n.d.). Your Happiness Guide, p. 10. Downloaded from https://laughteryoga.org/

Krznaric, R. (2012, November 27). Six habits of highly empathetic people. *Greater Good Magazine*. Retrieved from greatergood.berkeley.edu/article/item/six_habits_of_highly_empathic_people1

Lally, P., van Jaarsveld, C. H. M., Potts, H. W. W., & Wardle, J. (2010, October). How are habits formed: Modelling habit formation in the real world. *European Journal of Social Psychology, 40*(6), 998–1009. http://doi.org/10.1002/ejsp.674

Lieberman, C. (n.d.). How to have a healthier relationship with your phone. *Real Simple Magazine*. Retrieved from realsimple.com/work-life/technology/unplug-and-recharge

Literacy and Language Center Media (2016, April 29). The benefits of movement in the classroom. Retrieved from literacyandlanguagecenter.com/the-benefits-of-movement-in-the-classroom

Livni, E. (2018, May 27). Resilience is the new happiness. *Quartz*. Retrieved from qz.com/1289236/resilience-is-the-new-happiness

Lumsden, J., Miles, L. K., & Macrae, C. N. (2014). Sync or sink? Interpersonal synchrony impacts self-esteem. *Frontiers in Psychology, 5*, 1064. http://doi 10.3389/fpsyg.2014.01064

MacDonald, H. (2016, August 17). The practical benefits of a wandering mind. *Psychology Today*. Retrieved from https://www.psychologytoday.com/us/blog/time-travelling-apollo/201608/the-practical-benefits-wandering-mind

Mark, G. (2008, July 28) Worker interrupted: The cost of task switching/Interviewer: Kermit Pattison. *Fast Company*. Retrieved from fastcompany.com/944128/worker-interrupted-cost-task-switching

Morris, K. (2018, February 5). How to teach digital citizenship through blogging [Blog]. Retrieved from https://www.theedublogger.com/digital-citizenship-blogging/

Moser, L. (2016, April 12). Physical education in American schools is getting lapped. *Slate*. Retrieved from https://slate.com/human-interest/2016/04/most-states-are-shortchanging-kids-on-physical-education-study-finds.html

Myer, G. D., Faigenbaum, A. D., Edwards, N. M., Clark, J. F., Best, T. M., & Sallis, R. E. (2015). Sixty minutes of what? A developing brain perspective for activating children with an integrative exercise approach. *BJSM Online First*. Retrieved from https://blog.cincinnatichildrens.org/wp-content/uploads/2015/02/60-Minutes-of-What-in-BJSM.pdf

Oettingen, G. (2014). *Rethinking positive thinking: Inside the new science of motivation*. Shelton, CT: Current Publishing Inc.

Olderbak, S., Sassenrath, C., Keller, J., & Wilhelm, O. (2014, July 1). An emotion-differentiated perspective on empathy with the emotion specific empathy questionnaire. *Frontiers in Psychology*. Retrieved from https://doi.org/10.3389/fpsyg.2014.00653

Pachai, A. A., Acai, A., LoGiudice, A. B., & Kim, J. A. (2016, March). The mind that wanders: Challenges and potential benefits of mind wandering in education. *Scholarship of Teaching and Learning in Psychology, 2*(2), 134–46. Retrieved from http://dx.doi.org/10.1037/stl0000060

Pascha, M. (2017, February 24). The PERMA model: Your scientific theory of happiness. Retrieved from positivepsychologyprogram.com/perma-model

Pillay, S. (2016, March 28). How simply moving benefits your mental health [Blog]. *Harvard Health Publishing*. Retrieved from https://www.health.harvard.edu/blog/how-simply-moving-benefits-your-mental-health-201603289350

Pogue, D. (2017, August 20). Internet shaming: When mob justice goes virtual. *CBS News.* Retrieved from cbsnews.com/news/internet-shaming-when-mob-justice-goes-virtual

Porter, E. H. (1913). *Pollyanna.* Retrieved from gutenberg.org/ebooks/1450

Pritchard, M. (2013, January). Who are the Joneses and why are we trying to keep up with them? *HuffPost.* Retrieved from huffingtonpost.com/mary-pritchard/keeping-up-with-the-joneses_b_2467957.html

Proctor, M. (n.d.). Six science-backed ways being kind is good for your health [Blog]. Retrieved from quietrev.com/6-science-backed-ways-being-kind-is-good-for-your-health

Psychology Today. (n.d.). Positive psychology. Retrieved from psychologytoday.com/therapy-types/positive-psychology

Psychology Today. (n.d.). Resilience. Retrieved from psychologytoday.com/us/basics/resilience

Pychyl, T. (2008, April 15). Procrastination: A strategy for change. *Psychology Today.* Retrieved from https://www.psychologytoday.com/us/blog/dont-delay/200804/procrastination-strategy-change

Rosen, L., & Samuel, A. (2015, June). Conquering Digital Distraction. *Harvard Business Review.* Retrieved from https://hbr.org/2015/06/conquering-digital-distraction

Rosenberg, M., Confessore, N. & Cadwalladr, C. (2018, March 17). How Trump consultants exploited the Facebook data of millions. *New York Times.* Retrieved from nytimes.com/2018/03/17/us/politics/cambridge-analytica-trump-campaign.html

The RSA. (2013, December 10). *Brené Brown on empathy* [Video file]. Retrieved from https://www.youtube.com/watch?v=1Evwgu369Jw

Sharpe, M. (2017, July 13). Stoicism 5.0: The unlikely 21st century reboot of an ancient philosophy. *The Conversation.* Retrieved from http://theconversation.com/stoicism-5-0-the-unlikely-21st-century-reboot-of-an-ancient-philosophy-80986

Sifferlin, A. (2017, July 26). Here's how happy Americans are right now. *TIME.* Retrieved from time.com/4871720/how-happy-are-americans

Sisson, M. (2014, February 26). The best exercise there is, hands down. Retrieved from marksdailyapple.com/the-best-exercise-there-is-hands-down

Stevenson, P. (2006, July 24). Distractions make learning harder. *CBS News*. Retrieved from cbsnews.com/news/distractions-make-learning-harder

Suler, J. (2004). The online disinhibition effect. Retrieved from truecenterpublishing.com/psycyber/disinhibit.html

Suttie, J. (2018, February 14). How mind-wandering may be good for you. *Greater Good Magazine*. Retrieved from greatergood.berkeley.edu/article/item/how_mind_wandering_may_be_good_for_you

TEDx Talks. (2013, December 12). *The power of empathy: Helen Riess at TEDxMiddlebury* [Video file]. Retrieved from https://www.youtube.com/watch?v=baHrcC8B4WM&t=2s

Thibodeaux, W. (2018, March 22). Distractions are costing companies millions: Here's why 66 percent of workers won't talk about it. *Inc.5000*. Retrieved from https://www.inc.com/wanda-thibodeaux/new-survey-shows-70-percent-of-workers-feel-distracted-heres-why.html

Turkle, S. (2012, February). *Sherry Turkle: Connected but alone?* [Video file]. Retrieved from https://www.ted.com/talks/sherry_turkle_alone_together?language=en#t-656351

University of California - Los Angeles. (2006, July 26) Multi-tasking Adversely Affects Brain's Learning, UCLA Psychologists Report. *ScienceDaily*. Retrieved from www.sciencedaily.com/releases/2006/07/060726083302.htm

Vital, A. (n.d.). How not to be hard on yourself [Infographic]. *Happiness.com*. Retrieved from www.happiness.com/en/magazine/personal-growth/visual-guide-self-compassion/

Walker, C. (2009). *29 Gifts: How a month of giving can change your life.* Philadelphia, PA: Da Capo Press.

Westervelt, E. (2015, March 25). Learning to move, moving to learn: The benefits of PE. *NPR*. Retrieved from https://www.npr.org/sections/ed/2015/03/25/394346747/learning-to-move-and-moving-to-learn

Youmell, P. (n.d.) Twenty-three great reasons to exercise. Retrieved from paulayoumellrn.com/23-benefits-of-movement-exercise

ISTE Standards for Education Leaders

The ISTE Standards for Education Leaders guide administrators in supporting digital age learning, creating technology-rich learning environments and leading the transformation of the educational landscape.

1. Equity and Citizenship Advocate

Leaders use technology to increase equity, inclusion, and digital citizenship practices. Education leaders:

a. Ensure all students have skilled teachers who actively use technology to meet student learning needs.

b. Ensure all students have access to the technology and connectivity necessary to participate in authentic and engaging learning opportunities.

c. Model digital citizenship by critically evaluating online resources, engaging in civil discourse online and using digital tools to contribute to positive social change.

d. Cultivate responsible online behavior, including the safe, ethical and legal use of technology.

2. Visionary Planner

Leaders engage others in establishing a vision, strategic plan and ongoing evaluation cycle for transforming learning with technology. Education leaders:

a. Engage education stakeholders in developing and adopting a shared vision for using technology to improve student success, informed by the learning sciences.

b. Build on the shared vision by collaboratively creating a strategic plan that articulates how technology will be used to enhance learning.

c. Evaluate progress on the strategic plan, make course corrections, measure impact and scale effective approaches for using technology to transform learning.

d. Communicate effectively with stakeholders to gather input on the plan, celebrate successes and engage in a continuous improvement cycle.

e. Share lessons learned, best practices, challenges and the impact of learning with technology with other education leaders who want to learn from this work.

3. Empowering Leader

Leaders create a culture where teachers and learners are empowered to use technology in innovative ways to enrich teaching and learning. Education leaders:

a. Empower educators to exercise professional agency, build teacher leadership skills and pursue personalized professional learning.

b. Build the confidence and competency of educators to put the ISTE Standards for Students and Educators into practice.

c. Inspire a culture of innovation and collaboration that allows the time and space to explore and experiment with digital tools.

d. Support educators in using technology to advance learning that meets the diverse learning, cultural, and social-emotional needs of individual students.

e. Develop learning assessments that provide a personalized, actionable view of student progress in real time.

4. Systems Designer

Leaders build teams and systems to implement, sustain and continually improve the use of technology to support learning. Education leaders:

a. Lead teams to collaboratively establish robust infrastructure and systems needed to implement the strategic plan.

b. Ensure that resources for supporting the effective use of technology for learning are sufficient and scalable to meet future demand.

c. Protect privacy and security by ensuring that students and staff observe effective privacy and data management policies.

d. Establish partnerships that support the strategic vision, achieve learning priorities and improve operations.

5. Connected Learner

Leaders model and promote continuous professional learning for themselves and others. Education leaders:

a. Set goals to remain current on emerging technologies for learning, innovations in pedagogy and advancements in the learning sciences.

b. Participate regularly in online professional learning networks to collaboratively learn with and mentor other professionals.

c. Use technology to regularly engage in reflective practices that support personal and professional growth.

d. Develop the skills needed to lead and navigate change, advance systems and promote a mindset of continuous improvement for how technology can improve learning.

ISTE Standards for Educators

The ISTE Standards for Educators are your road map to helping students become empowered learners. These standards will deepen your practice, promote collaboration with peers, challenge you to rethink traditional approaches and prepare students to drive their own learning.

Empowered Professional

1. Learner

Educators continually improve their practice by learning from and with others and exploring proven and promising practices that leverage technology to improve student learning. Educators:

a. Set professional learning goals to explore and apply pedagogical approaches made possible by technology and reflect on their effectiveness.

b. Pursue professional interests by creating and actively participating in local and global learning networks.

c. Stay current with research that supports improved student learning outcomes, including findings from the learning sciences.

2. Leader

Educators seek out opportunities for leadership to support student empowerment and success and to improve teaching and learning. Educators:

a. Shape, advance and accelerate a shared vision for empowered learning with technology by engaging with education stakeholders.

b. Advocate for equitable access to educational technology, digital content and learning opportunities to meet the diverse needs of all students.

c. Model for colleagues the identification, exploration, evaluation, curation and adoption of new digital resources and tools for learning.

3. Citizen

Educators inspire students to positively contribute to and responsibly participate in the digital world. Educators:

a. Create experiences for learners to make positive, socially responsible contributions and exhibit empathetic behavior online that build relationships and community.

b. Establish a learning culture that promotes curiosity and critical examination of online resources and fosters digital literacy and media fluency.

c. Mentor students in safe, legal and ethical practices with digital tools and the protection of intellectual rights and property.

d. Model and promote management of personal data and digital identity and protect student data privacy.

Learning Catalyst

4. Collaborator

Educators dedicate time to collaborate with both colleagues and students to improve practice, discover and share resources and ideas, and solve problems. Educators:

a. Dedicate planning time to collaborate with colleagues to create authentic learning experiences that leverage technology.

b. Collaborate and co-learn with students to discover and use new digital resources and diagnose and troubleshoot technology issues.

c. Use collaborative tools to expand students' authentic, real-world learning experiences by engaging virtually with experts, teams and students, locally and globally.

d. Demonstrate cultural competency when communicating with students, parents and colleagues and interact with them as co-collaborators in student learning.

5. Designer

Educators design authentic, learner-driven activities and environments that recognize and accommodate learner variability. Educators:

a. Use technology to create, adapt and personalize learning experiences that foster independent learning and accommodate learner differences and needs.

b. Design authentic learning activities that align with content area standards and use digital tools and resources to maximize active, deep learning.

c. Explore and apply instructional design principles to create innovative digital learning environments that engage and support learning.

6. Facilitator

Educators facilitate learning with technology to support student achievement of the 2016 ISTE Standards for Students. Educators:

    a. Foster a culture where students take ownership of their learning goals and outcomes in both independent and group settings.

    b. Manage the use of technology and student learning strategies in digital platforms, virtual environments, hands-on makerspaces or in the field.

    c. Create learning opportunities that challenge students to use a design process and computational thinking to innovate and solve problems.

    d. Model and nurture creativity and creative expression to communicate ideas, knowledge or connections.

7. Analyst

Educators understand and use data to drive their instruction and support students in achieving their learning goals. Educators:

    a. Provide alternative ways for students to demonstrate competency and reflect on their learning using technology.

    b. Use technology to design and implement a variety of formative and summative assessments that accommodate learner needs, provide timely feedback to students and inform instruction.

    c. Use assessment data to guide progress and communicate with students, parents and education stakeholders to build student self-direction.

Index

Your opinion matters:
Tell us how we're doing!

Your feedback helps ISTE create the best possible resources for teaching and learning in the digital age. Share your thoughts with the community or tell us how we're doing!

You can:

- **Write a review at amazon.com or barnesandnoble.com.**

- **Follow ISTE on these channels:**

Twitter @iste   Facebook @ISTEconnects   Instagram @isteconnects

- **Email us at books@iste.org with your questions or comments.**